PTSD

How Overcoming Anxiety, Depression, and PTSD Taught Me the Power of *Pushing Toward Success Daily*

SHANNON LOMBARD
WITH STEPHANIE LOMBARD

SIGNATURE

27 26 25   24   23   22   21   1   2   3   4   5   6

PTSD: How Overcoming Anxiety Depression and PTSD Taught Me the
Power of Pushing Toward Success Daily
Copyright ©2021 Shannon Lombard, Stephanie Lombard

Published by:
Signature Media, llc
4770 Eureka Ave.
Yorba Linda, CA 92885
www.signature.pub

Library of Congress Cataloging-in-Publication Data:
ISBN: 978-1-949758-67-2 Paperback
ISBN: 978-1-949758-59-7 Digital/E-book

BISAC Category:
SEL043000   SELF-HELP / Post-Traumatic Stress Disorder (PTSD)
PSY022040   PSYCHOLOGY / Post-Traumatic Stress Disorder
HEA039110   HEALTH & FITNESS / Diseases / Nervous System

CONTENTS

DEDICATION

This book is dedicated to Nina-Boo,
Papa Deux, and Mommy.

Thank you for believing in Daddy.

We are the Fearless Foursome.

ACKNOWLEDGMENTS

No one who achieves success does so without acknowledging the help of others. The wise and confident acknowledge this help with gratitude.

- Alfred North Whitehead -

I know I would not be in the position I am in today without the help of some significant people that have been or still are a part of my life. It is essential always to give thanks and acknowledge those individuals who take the time to love, support, and be there for you. It is human nature to want to be recognized for individual efforts that are made for others, and I will always find the time to say thank you when and how often I can.

Mom and Dad, you two are the epitome of love and support. I know that I have not always been the perfect kid, but I appreciate you giving me the space to figure out what I needed to see with my own eyes and pulling hard on the rope when I needed that too. You gave me the proper foundation required to never stray far from home, and I cannot say thank you enough for that. We never wanted anything as kids because you showed us what hard work looked like without the lectures and long talks. I saw firsthand that actions speak louder than words. Now you are the best grandparents that we could have ever imagined. I pray to make you proud of what I look to accomplish, no matter how crazy it might sound to you! I love you for what you have put in me and on my heart.

Mic and Meg, you are the best siblings a big brother can have. I may not have always been the easiest to talk with or be around, but you still have stuck it out with me all of these years. I see the hard work and vision in both of you and will continue to support you in all of your endeavors. Love you two. Jo, it is because of you that we lasted this long. We appreciate you being our sounding/yelling board when we need you. As we usually say, "You cannot be mad. You did this."

Chuck and Paula, I appreciate the young woman you two raised. She has been such a blessing to so many people, which should make you abundantly proud. I appreciate you allowing me her hand in marriage to build our family we have today. Thank you and Charles for the support for us and the kids who love you very much.

To all of my brothers and sisters in arms: active duty, guard, reservists, KIA, POW, and military veterans. What you do daily to protect our rights as U.S. citizens is something that I understand and salute you for. It is because of your bravery I can sit here in peace and pour my life story on paper. I have made some life-long friends during and after my tenure as an airman. Josh, Ian, Rory, you guys helped me be a man, and stay one, while never losing my true self and childish exuberance about life. Thanks for making me see other parts of the world and lasting friendships.

My biggest goal in life was achieved when I received the invitation phone call from the city of Los Angeles Fire Department. It was there I found my new tribe of brave men and women who give their lives daily in the service of strangers. They are the type of people who would not have it any other way. I thank you for the love and support over the seven-plus years that I was able to call you all brothers and sisters. To my immediate family within my most prominent family: Ken, Kev, Tek, and KB. We all had each other's backs from the day that we walked into the academy and the great unknown. The love and support I got from you guys through the academy and beyond I will never forget. Thank you.

My westside family with Eric, Jay, Aaron, Mike, and Adam. You guys laughed, ate, slept, fought, sacrificed, and loved me for the better part of my career. The bond we built in those years together is unmatched in my life beyond my blood relatives, and I want to thank you from the bottom of my heart for keeping me safe and allowing me to get back home to my family every morning.

Sam, you were the first one to open our eyes to the possibilities of a life lived bigger. I thank you for giving us a chance to realize a dream we did not know we had by opening our first business. You pushed, challenged, moved, and, most importantly, supported us throughout our entrepreneur journey and are still only one text or call away. We appreciate what you have done for our family and us. The lasting impact that you have had on our goals, vision, and dreams is something that I cannot measure in words. Thank you, Brother, for everything.

To our team at Signature Media: Stefan, Christian, and Tim. I cannot describe the support that you have shown me through this book-writing process. I had zero clue on how to write a book, but I knew what I wanted to say. That was enough for you guys to take this project on, and I am forever grateful for the opportunity to reach more people with this story of hope and support in a world that truly needs it.

With your help, this book has a chance to be an inspiration to many people, and I thank you once again for believing in me and, most importantly, my story.

Nina Sophia (AKA Nina Boo) and Shannon Paul-Emil (AKA Papa Deux): the love I have for you both is more profound than the ocean and more significant than space! Daddy will continue to work hard for you to see the world with a look of love, compassion, and joy. I am so proud of what you have accomplished so far, and you continue to make me laugh and enjoy every second I get to spend with you two. Daddy loves you so very much!

Stephanie Michelle Lombard, you are the reason and inspiration for this book. I am forever indebted to you for running, crawling, crying, yelling, laughing, with me and never leaving my side throughout this season in my life. Your persistence and vision inspire me daily to do everything in my power to push us to higher heights as a couple and as a family. I am happy that I asked you to spend the rest of your life with me. We are going to keep pushing ourselves and each other to get better mentally, physically, and spiritually. God has our back because we are asking for it together. I love you until my last day and beyond.

FOREWORD

Demons never go away on their own, they don't just decide to leave us alone one day. It's a daily fight, and they always fight back. This fight can ruin a marriage, a career, a family, everything you've built. But it's a fight that must be had.

Shannon knew this better than anyone, he sensed it, his gut was telling him to act. Few people have the courage to do that, especially with all of life's pressures. We can be overwhelmed by so many things that we just stay living in something that hurts us and will continue to hurt us. It comes down to this: Are you willing to let go of what you have, to fight for what you really want.

That's what Shannon did. He left a dream career, stability, safety, in pursuit of something greater. It didn't matter how many times he heard that he was making the wrong choice, or that he was going to fail. All he saw was the life he knew he could have and had a relentless pursuit towards it.

If you want a better life, if you know there's more out there, Shannon will help you get it. This man didn't study it, didn't read about it, he lived it. If you want that too, this book is the first step.

Dr. Saman Bakhtiar
CEO The Camp Transformation Centers Int'l.

MY STORY

Hi, my name is Shannon and I was diagnosed with depression, anxiety and Post-traumatic Stress Disorder (PTSD). There, I said it. It's also what this book is about. Before my diagnosis, I was a passionate full-time firefighter, an attentive husband, and present father. I had worked hard for years to finally land my dream job in the Los Angeles Fire Department. I had the perfect marriage and happy kids. In every way, I was living my American Dream.

Then one day, everything began to change. The pressures of my job started to add up and affect me in a different way. In turn, I started acting differently, responding to stress differently, and treating my wife and kids differently. Getting PTSD didn't happen all at once. There was no defining moment where I didn't have it and then I did. Instead, it was subtle. The symptoms were initially small and became worse over time.

As I began to unravel, so did the rest of my life. The more I suffered, the more my marriage suffered. The angrier I felt, the angrier my kids got me. Eventually, I found my life in shambles—my marriage two steps away from divorce, my kids hating my guts—and I was emotionally and psychologically unable to put things back together.

My illness caused by my stress at work forced me to make the biggest decision of my life. Do I keep my dream job as a firefighter, or do I quit, get help, and save my family? The moment I understood the choice was also the moment I knew the answer. At 36 years old and now diagnosed with PTSD, I quit my job, hit the reset button on my life, and began the long journey of recovery. The next three years were the hardest three years of my life. Learning to manage PTSD proved a harder task than marriage, fatherhood, my time in the military, and the demands of my career. It was taxing, relentless, exhausting, and stressful. It required me to search my soul, take inventory of my present, come to terms with my past, and rethink my future. It meant throwing out the life playbook my wife and I had written and starting all over again. This is my story of how I, and my family, overcame PTSD and how I think you and your loved ones can too.

A Young Boy's Dream

I knew I wanted to become a firefighter when I was 14 years old. My parents let me enroll in a Junior Firefighter

Explorer program in a city not too far from where I lived. I remember how excited I was when I heard the news I had been accepted. It would be my first taste of what being a real firefighter would be like. It also gave me a strong sense of purpose that felt qualitatively more important than just being involved in just another sport or extracurricular activity. **For me, at that moment, being accepted meant everything**. My father—who gave me the idea to sign up in the first place—seemed as excited about it as I was.

The one-year program had an incredible effect on me and the trajectory of my life. First, it gave me an inside look at what it would take physically and mentally to overcome the dangers of fighting fires. Second, it also stoked a burning desire in me to dedicate my life to fighting fires and helping people in need. By the time I graduated, I knew exactly what I wanted to do. When I grew up—I knew for certain—I was going to become a firefighter.

The Journey Begins

Four years after my Junior Firefighter experience, I joined the military at 18 years old. When I signed up, I had every intention of becoming a military firefighter. The first time I applied to the program, I was denied because the fire academy was full. That bummed me out. Even so, I knew that, before my military career was over, I was going to achieve my goal of becoming a military firefighter. Eventually, I was given the chance, and I became one.

After serving my country for close to six years, and working and traveling for four more years, I moved back home to Los Angeles and immediately applied to become a firefighter for the City of Los Angeles. I still remember the day I got the acceptance call like it was yesterday. For me, being chosen to serve was like being drafted into the major leagues. In February of 2009, I walked into the Los Angeles Fire Department Academy to start my first day of training. At 27 years old, I had just achieved my biggest goal in life. I was finally in a position to begin to fulfill my calling.

When people have asked me what my plan B is, I've always responded, "To refer back to plan A." For my entire life, I have never had a plan B for anything. Nor do I expect I ever will. Why? A contingency plan, in my mind, is the first step to allowing defeat. I took the same outlook toward my career path. My dream was to be a firefighter. So that's all I planned and worked toward being. To spend time doing anything else was a waste of time.

A Life Interruption

For the next seven years, working for the Los Angeles Fire Department was an incredible experience. I was seven years into what was supposed to be a thirty-year career before my illness began to affect my life. My wife, whom I met before my career with the LAFD, and I have two beautiful kids who were ages one and two at the time. My wife worked seven miles from home. I was in school full-time, working toward my bachelor's degree. We had just opened up our first business together, which was a fitness facility that we wound up building into a multiple seven-figure business. We were hustling, moving, and making things happen.

As quickly as this paragraph changed, so did my state of mind. Even though my symptoms developed over time, there was a part of my PTSD experience that felt like it happened overnight. One day, I was gone. Even though I was still functioning, my feelings began to shut down and operate on a different frequency than before. Regardless of the weather outside, for me, the sun wasn't shining anymore. I went from the highest highs to the lowest lows, and there was nothing I could do to stop it.

My isolated feelings of depression began to bleed over into all aspects of my thought life. One of my accomplishments I am most PROUD of was receiving my bachelor's degree in business organizational management. As I worked toward my degree, even though I intellectually knew what I was doing was good, emotionally I felt nothing except sadness. Every feeling, thought, and action was clouded. No good experience could escape the darkness that followed. No positive thought could last in the anxiety and depression that was constant.

The realities of anxiety and depression completely changed my personality and my actions with it. I became emotionally cut off from others. That led to outbursts of rage and anger. Eventually, my emotional and psychological state began to actively sabotage my marriage and the stability of my family. All aspects of my life became interrupted.

My Diagnosis

When I was first told that I was diagnosed with PTSD, anxiety, and depression, it felt like I was handed three consecutive life sentences. In my current state, life had already become unbearable. I could not control my emotions. I could not stand being around my family. I could not even bring myself to smile and laugh most days. For me, that was the most alarming because that is not the type of individual I am. My comfort zone had shifted entirely. My wife and I had designed our lives to be each other's best friend, and at that point, we were our own worst enemies. My kids could not stand being around me, and if you are a parent reading this, you can imagine the feeling that I had.

After hearing the doctor say the word PTSD, there were innumerable questions that flooded my mind at the same time. I had heard the term before but did not know what it really was. I did not know the symptoms or how to treat it. I wasn't even fully confident I knew what the acronym stood for. "At least," I thought, "I know what it is." That was my silver lining. A diagnosis is a start. If there was a name, that must have meant my doctor knew what it was. If doctors knew what it was, maybe there was a chance there was a way to cure it.

When a Dream Dies

I remember my last day as a firefighter. It wasn't long after my official PTSD diagnosis. I remember walking out a door that tens of thousands of men and women who also served as firefighters walk through every year. But unlike them, today would be my last day walking through as a firefighter. It was the most difficult door I have ever walked through in my life. Why? Because it came with accepting that the dream of my life had died.

Choosing to resign from firefighting only at thirty-six was not a decision that came lightly. That said, my diagnosis had forced me into a situation where I had to make a decision. For years, I had seen other soldiers, firefighters, and police officers ignore the demands and side effects of the job and how that decision, too often, destroyed families. I knew early on that wasn't a choice I was willing to make. I loved being a firefighter more than anything. Except being a good father to my kids and loving husband to my wife. If I was going to have a shot at putting my marriage and my family back together, it had to start with me being willing to make the sacrifice required.

A New Dream is Born

Even though my diagnosis was incredibly hard to face, in hindsight, it was the best decision I ever made. Even though I had lost my dream, the choice to take ownership and responsibility would pave the way for my recovery and the recovery of our family.

Not long after, I woke up in the morning, tired of being tired. I told myself, "I have to change my story." If things were going to be different, I knew I had to make a *choice,* and it was a *choice* I would have to make daily. If I wanted a future, I had to find a new future. If I was going to successfully overcome my illness, I would have to be willing to do the work. I'd have to have the guts to stay steady, to fix myself, and press forward no matter how long it took or in how little increments I could muster.

I can tell you from personal experience, the choice to change your story can be the difference that can lead you out of the deep, dark hole you might feel that you're in. For me, it took me a year of self-encouragement and therapy before I began to achieve results. With a lot of work, eventually, I changed my story. Over time, I went from *suffering* from PTSD to *living* with PTSD. I got there because I learned the power of **Pushing Toward Success Daily.**

One Step at a Time

There will always be a moment in life when you begin to receive the rewards of past decisions and actions. It's similar to the idea of sowing and reaping. Eventually, you will always reap what you sow. If you are making progress in inches, eventually it adds up to a foot, then a yard, and finally a mile. Your progress can also be different on different days. Sometimes you'll gain a foot, and other days you'll move the needle just one millimeter. Ultimately, if you harness the power of Pushing Toward Success Daily, you will have an accumulation of dividends. It is the compounding effect of small victories that will ultimately lead you to big rewards. I beat PTSD not with one big action or one incredible therapy session but through a series of small steps over a long time. I learned that if I wanted to recover, it would take me committing to ***Pushing Toward Success Daily.*** If I could just win today—even in a small way—I could win tomorrow. If I could win a little today and tomorrow, I would eventually win big the following day. I would be able to defeat my illness.

What PTSD Taught Me

Let me break down what PTSD taught me about the power of ***Pushing Toward Success Daily.*** Pushing means to move. Whether it is one millimeter or one mile, you must move every day. Do something that makes you happy every day, no matter how big or how small. Toward means you are focused on a goal and/or vision for your life. You have to tell yourself every day that you will not stay stagnant. You will not stay focused on where you are but where you want to be. Every day means one step closer to your goals in life. Success is something that I push for every day. Going to the gym and moving your body can be measured as a success for the day. Bringing my kids to school is a success for that day. A hug and a kiss from my wife can be considered progress for that day. <u>D</u>aily means just what it says. Every. Single. Day.

Why I Wrote This Book

I wrote this book because I want to encourage others who suffer from anxiety, depression, or PTSD that they can make it too. I hope by sharing my story and some of those lessons I've learned, you can also harness the power of ***<u>P</u>ushing <u>T</u>oward <u>S</u>uccess <u>D</u>aily*** in your own life.

My journey from *"suffering from"* to *"living with"* PTSD was long and hard. Even though it was filled with misery, it ultimately led to one of the most profound periods of growth in my life and made me the man I am today. I am here to tell you today, "What does not kill you *will* make you stronger." If you are a person suffering from stress, anxiety, depression, or PTSD, there are only two ways out:

1) You either let it take YOU out

OR

2) You take IT out

I am here to tell you that you can make it too. Everything I have written in this book I have learned through trial and error. I hope this four-step system helps you rewrite your story as much as it helped me rewrite mine. If you're willing to discover what the power of **_Pushing Toward Success Daily_** can do for you, get ready! The first step along your journey to re-create a fruitful and meaningful life begins now!

S.O.S.: HOUSTON, WE HAVE A PROBLEM

There is nothing worse in life than the feeling of betrayal. It does not matter where it comes from. Even if you betray yourself, it still hurts just as much as if it were someone else. My mind regularly betrayed my body. I often felt like the astronauts in the Apollo 13 space mission who were stuck in a spaceship that wasn't working properly. **"Houston, we have a problem!"** I would tell myself. I did not have the words to describe how I felt, but I knew deep down that something was not right.

For most of my life, I had felt invincible. I was on top of the world. I felt utterly indestructible, both mentally and physically. Then one day, all of that changed. It was as if a Trojan horse appeared in the middle of my impenetrable fortress overnight. It came fast. It came on strong, and it came without warning. I felt as if I had no control over my words, my emotions, or my actions. I knew that something was wrong, and yet I felt trapped in my mind and could not get out.

What made the situation worse was that there was never an isolated incident I could point to where things changed. The betrayal was gradual, affecting every part of me. Similar to how code can be rewritten in a computer, I felt like someone or something was rewriting who I was. My life as I knew it fell apart, and as I shut down, all other parts of my life followed. The house looked like a wreck. I no longer kept a schedule, which resulted in me not having anything to work toward. I began to be awake at odd hours of the night and slept in until late in the day. When I say that I could not think straight, I mean that with sincerity. I knew something was wrong. I felt like I was sick. Nothing I tried on my own could change it. My breakthrough came when I decided to get help, understand my disorder, and Push Toward Success Daily.

The Destructive Power of PTSD, Anxiety, and Depression

- **PTSD** is a disorder in which a person has difficulty recovering after experiencing or witnessing a terrifying event. It's an order that affects roughly 3.5 percent of U.S. adults. An estimated one in eleven people will be diagnosed with PTSD in their lifetime. Women are twice as likely as men to have PTSD. Seventy percent of adults experience at least one traumatic event in their lifetime. Twenty percent of people who experience a traumatic event will develop PTSD. About eight million people have PTSD in a given year according to the Anxiety and Depression Association of America.

- *Anxiety* is a mental health disorder that often accompanies PTSD. It is characterized by feelings of worry, anxiety, or fear that are strong enough to interfere with one's daily activities. According to the Anxiety and Depression Association of America, **anxiety** disorders are the most common mental illness in the U.S., affecting forty million adults in the United States age 18 and older, or 18.1 percent of the population every year. Anxiety disorders are highly treatable, yet only 36.9 percent of those suffering receive treatment.

- *Depression* is a mental health disorder characterized by persistently depressed mood or loss of interest in activities, causing significant impairment in daily life. According to the Anxiety and Depression Association of America, **depression** is the leading cause of disability in the U.S. for ages 15 to 44. Major depressive disorder affects more than 16.1 million American adults, or about

6.7 percent of the U.S. population age 18 and older, in a given year. While major depressive disorder can develop at any age, the median age at onset is 32.5 years old. It is more prevalent in women than in men.

- *Stress* is a feeling of emotional or physical tension. It can come from any event or thought that makes you feel frustrated, angry, or nervous. **Stress** is your body's reaction to a challenge or demand. According to the American Institute for Stress, about 33 percent of people report feeling extreme stress. Seventy-seven percent of people experience stress that affects their physical health. Seventy-three percent of people have stress that impacts their mental health. Forty-eight percent of people have trouble sleeping because of stress. People who tend to experience particularly high rates of stress include:

    - Ethnic minorities
    - Women
    - Single parents
    - People responsible for their family's health-care decisions

Today, over seventy million people suffer from one of these mental health disorders in the U.S. alone. That number is not only staggering, but it is also climbing. The first lesson I learned in my diagnosis was that I was not alone, and if you or someone you love is suffering from one or more of these diseases, then you aren't either. It may feel like you are alone more often than not, but that is a part of what these illnesses do: make you feel isolated and helpless. I remember how I felt about being diagnosed. **Alone. Terrified. Confused. Tormented. Questioning. Angry. Abandoned. Bitter. Disoriented.** And that was just by morning.

As I dealt with my inward emotions, I had external expressions of my illness that everyone else could see that I initially tried to explain away.

I Self-Isolated

My favorite days were when the house was empty, and the silence was deafening. It was easier to be alone. Those days were the most peaceful and yet challenging days of my life. My couch was my safety zone and my TV was my best friend. I have always been the outdoors type of individual, hence my career choices. It would be 80° and not a cloud in the sky outside, but inside the house, I had the shutters closed, and the air conditioning turned on full blast. I would be hiding under a blanket in the middle of a Tuesday. That was when my soul felt the emptiest. Those were the days I suffered the most. The feeling of being trapped would become overwhelming. No matter what I did, I couldn't get out of my head. This is a symptom that I eventually discovered later in my journey for healing is called self-isolation.

As FHEHealth states, "Self-isolation refers to the tendency to separate oneself from others. Rather than going to parties, taking part in team events, hanging out with friends or spending time with family members, individuals will instead choose to spend time alone.

"While it's normal for everyone to crave solo time on occasion, self-isolation goes far beyond forgoing a few events. Those who self-isolate completely retreat into themselves, allowing the stress involved in seeing others and taking part in normal activities to prevent participation in previously pleasurable behaviors.

"Self-isolation can be a symptom of other forms of mental illness, like <u>depression</u> or <u>anxiety disorders</u>, but is a key side effect to note in those living with PTSD.[1]"

I Had Intense Nightmares

I was having night terrors seemingly every night that I was sleeping in my own bed. Some nights, Stephanie would have to pull me out of my nightmare, literally, and talk me through where I was and that everything would be ok. I was waking up consistently with soaking wet sheets and total confusion. I will be honest and say that it was even during the days and nights where it had been a better day than most. I was not watching anything on TV that was triggering any thoughts in my mind nor was I going to sleep angry.

---

[1] Chris Foy, "The Reasons Your Loved One with PTSD is Self-solating." August 29, 2019 **https://fherehab.com/learning/reasons-ptsd-self-isolating/**

There were no specific nightmares that I was having consistently either. I tried listening to calming meditative music that would last a couple minutes because I assumed it would not work. I stayed awake as long as my eyes would remain open and figured if I fell asleep that way it would make a difference. I cannot say I tried EVERYTHING, but I attempted a few prior-to-sleeping exercises, and none of them had a positive effect on me at the time. That led to the insomnia which would be a huge challenge for me as well. I felt too afraid to sleep because of possible nightmares, which resulted in me being awake all night. Then my next day was a blur because I would be so tired. At work, however, I was too tired and wired to feel like I was asleep anyway, so I never experienced any issues there. It was only in my "safe space" at home. **I was suffering in the day and at night.**

Sleep.org explains that, "Anyone can experience nightmares or night terrors, but as many as 96% of people with posttraumatic stress disorder (PTSD) suffer from vivid nightmares that can feel overwhelmingly real. And unlike garden-variety bad dreams, those nightmares are more likely to involve physical thrashing or other bodily movements. For some, that can make sleeping in the same bed difficult, if not dangerous." [2]

I Would Get Uncontrollably Angry

My daily battle with rage and anger was constant. I felt like a stick of dynamite whose fuse was on autopilot at all times. It did not matter what time, place, people, situation, etc.; if something set me off, then I would address it right then and there. It led to some pretty embarrassing events and situations for myself and my wife as the main receiver of my rage. For me, the anger was always on the surface searching for someone to rub me the wrong way. When a trigger finally happened, rage would push my anger to the side and take over to finish what was started. I have experienced rage and anger on a level that is utterly unexplainable, and at the time, I had no desire to harness it and get on the positive side of things.

If I was able to take that negative energy that was pouring out of my body on a consistent basis and redirect it to a more positive outlet, I would definitely have mastered a few things in life by now. Fluent Spanish, classical piano,

---

[2] "How to Deal with a Spouse Who Has PTSD Nightmares," Sleep.org, 2020. https://www.sleep.org/articles/deal-with-spouse-ptsd-nightmares/

master scuba diver, etc. Instead I channeled it at my wife, kids, and family. I was a "saint" at our business and in my career because I knew the implications if I was to let it out for others to see. There were no consequences in my mind to utterly unleash on Stephanie every chance I felt she deserved it. Or the kids for making a miniscule mistake as toddlers. In my mind, it was either to isolate myself to contain the anger and rage or risk being out at a family gathering and just hope it all went well.

It wasn't just verbal and mental anger either. **It just felt so good to put my hands on something beautiful to destroy it.** Zero thoughts or emotion behind it. No implications in my mind. I needed to unleash, and it was going to happen. There is a reason our master bedroom door does not match any of the other doors in our home. It is not by choice.

I Drank A Lot

It was nothing for me to have a drink at 9 a.m. The kids were gone, my wife was working, and I was left to my own devices. Scrambled eggs, hash browns, toast, side of bacon, and wash it all down with vodka and orange juice, aka a screwdriver. In my life, I would think that it was orange juice with a splash of vodka when it was actually the other way around. That one drink would lead to two, which would lead to three, until I was passed out on the couch. I slept until around lunchtime, got up, and grabbed a bite, and poured another drink.

I would let the kids stay with my mom until the same time my wife would get off work or come home from building our business. I would stop drinking just to where I was somewhat coherent, and as soon as she walked in the door, I would offer her a drink because that was the perfect excuse for me to have another one. Every night out, every meal out, every day with friends, and every chance I got, I was looking for the 80 proof. Holidays I always had a drink in my hand.

Alcohol was absolutely a coping mechanism. For most of my life, this was not the norm. Even when it became the norm, I knew excessive drinking wasn't me. I always told myself, "I don't have an addictive personality, so I can stop whenever I want to." That was my excuse. I never bothered to ask myself: why, despite me not being an addict, did I need a drink every day? That was the question I was avoiding.

When you are living like this every day, it will make you feel like you are going nuts especially because it may be so far out of the normal for you, just like me. I was so far gone

I felt like I was living on my own planet for half of the time, and the other time, I was building a business, working toward my bachelors' degree, and being a full-time professional firefighter. I was splitting my mental energy and emotions right down the middle, and I had no idea how to handle it.

If you are reading this and unknowingly nodding your head about yourself or someone you know, you or they are probably not managing the overall issue correctly. We talked about

- anger/rage
- self-isolation
- nightmares/night terrors
- insomnia
- coping with alcohol

One of the most common things about people who deal with stress, anxiety, depression, and PTSD is that they make excuses in regard to their behavior and it can be pretty easy for them to continue using those excuses. One of the first things that happens with individuals who deal with these mental health issues is denial. Denial comes with negative consequences that impact the person as well as the people closest to them. I had my own bout with this.

You know you are in denial when…

Your actions, attitude, and behavior pattern are out of your normal state of mind. Then you need to take a step back and recognize what and why you have changed. Denial is a part of not acknowledging the differences in your attitude, moods, and reactions. When your choices and behaviors are destructive, you are in denial about what you are doing to yourself and what you are partaking in. People who are struggling with mental health do not see anything wrong with how they are speaking to others or their reaction patterns and wonder why no one will just leave them alone. These are a few phrases that are often stated by those individuals who are in denial about the issues that they are facing on a daily basis.

- *"I am not angry; you just keep telling me I am angry."*
- *"I am not self- isolating; I just want to be alone. All day. Every day."*
- *"I don't need another drink; I just want one."*

The moment that I recognized and acknowledged that I was in denial was when things shifted for me. That was my first step in the direction of change for my life. Acknowledgement. This is what led me on my journey to Push Toward Success Daily.

STEP ONE: PUSH

Move Out of Your Comfort Zone
+ Get Help

I love the 1990's film *The Hunt for Red October*[3]. The plot of the movie centers around a Russian submarine captain, Marko Ramius (played by Sean Connery), who decides to go rogue and leads his crew into international waters toward the United States. As his submarine, the Red October, is tracked, in one scene, it's fired upon. Just missing their craft, the torpedo explodes right beside them, sending alarm bells ringing throughout the hull and many of the submarine systems going haywire. The scene is a perfect image of how a life interruption can often leave us scrambling in place. Often when one part of our life falls apart, it sets off a chain reaction that affects all of our life. Like the crew in the submarine, one alarm turns into all alarms warning us that all systems have failed. When this happens, it can be hard to know what to do first. It can be

---

[3] John McTiernan, *The Hunt for Red October*, Paramount Pictures, 2 March, 1990

hard to know how to respond when everything is falling apart at the same time.

<u>Responding to Red Flags</u>

One of the first things that people do if they're struggling with anxiety, depression, or PTSD is begin to do what I call red flag behavior. Red flag behavior often begins in the form of a coping mechanism. It doesn't matter who you are, what you do, or where you live, life is sometimes stressful—for everyone! Often the way we deal with that stress is through coping mechanisms. For the average person, coping mechanisms are pretty healthy. Granted, some are healthier than others. Common coping mechanisms include:

- Working out after a long day
- Having an extra glass of wine at dinner to unwind
- Watching a movie with a friend or loved one
- Doing yoga
- Eating a good meal

For someone dealing with anxiety, depression, or PTSD, simple, harmless coping mechanisms can often turn into extreme destructive behavior. They can begin to overdrink and over isolate. The excess stress and anxiety they are suffering from doesn't just stop increasing the extreme nature of their existing ways of dealing with stress. The stress will implode them and eventually spill over to every area of their life.

In fact, red flag behavior will almost always lead to total system overload and eventually total system failure. Overdrinking will quickly turn into binge drinking, drinking during the day, not sleeping, not having a schedule, and drinking at work. The system breakdowns will continue to compound until, eventually, a person has no schedule, no relationships, and no regular sleeping or eating habits. That's a complete system failure when a red flag behavior turns all alarm bells ringing. Something is clearly wrong and the ship is going down in a hurry.

It's Time to Start Pushing

When all systems are failing, the first thing you have to do to put your life back on track is make the commitment to start *pushing*. To push means to move, to exert force upon an object, whether it is movable or not. If you are suffering from anxiety, depression, stress, or PTSD, you're going to have to be willing to *push* to work yourself out the hole. That means pushing against red flag behaviors and putting your life back together one failed system at a time.

PUSH- to exert force on (someone or something), typically with one's hand, in order to move them away from oneself or the origin of the force.[4]

Think of a physical gym workout. If you are looking to tone your quadriceps, you are going to focus on lower body exercises for at least twenty minutes a day three to four days a week. You are probably going to increase your protein intake and lift heavier weights because you are working on a focused area of your body. Then you know you have to counterbalance that with an upper body workout, since it may look funny to have big legs and scrawny arms! **It is all about creating balances within your activities that are only going to benefit your overall results.**

Just like your physical health, with your mental health you have to start by setting up the plan. The plan is your PUSH. You are now working and moving every single day to accomplish this goal that you have set up. Dealing with

---

[4] "Push," Dictionary.com, Accessed 16 May 2020, https://www.dictionary.com/browse/push

stress, depression, anxiety, and PTSD is a game of pushing yourself past what you think you know because you are clearly not handling this the proper way.

These are the four areas that you will need to get ahold of and PUSH back:

1) Get out of your comfort zone/do something new
2) Set and keep a consistent schedule
3) Build your community
4) Get help

Get Out of Your Comfort Zone/Do Something New

Sometimes in life, you have to do something you've never done before to get somewhere you've never been before.

-Tim Storey-

I have always thought of myself as being a happy-go-lucky guy. Naturally, I gravitated toward the good, not the bad. I am the type of person who smiles before frowning. Life has always been one big ball of fun for me. Positivity is my natural default state of being, so when these new thoughts and gremlins began to invade my brain, I did not know how to handle it. The negative self-talk was overwhelming to say the least. I was so entrenched in my negativity; it was oozing from my pores. "You punk!" "What do you mean you can't handle it?" "They are functioning just fine but look at you." "I always knew you were soft." "What are Steph and the kids going to think now?" It is hard even reliving and typing those types of comments.

This is the issue of self-stigma that plagues many people who are struggling with their mental health. It is the constant negative feelings and emotions that do not allow you to see past the current situation you are in, and therefore, it makes it seemingly impossible to allow yourself the opportunity to achieve your mental well-being. Self-stigma destroys self-esteem and dissuades you from achieving life goals that were set. It can and will impede you from your ability to recover from any mental health issues.

Most people are afraid to recognize, acknowledge, and get the proper treatment to manage their everyday emotional and mental well-being. By getting uncomfortable, you create an opportunity to get your life back on the right track. Because you are willing to push out of your comfort zone, you can have more clarity on what kind of plan to make and what steps to take to get better. You may have told yourselves so much negative crap in the past that it is hard to see through your current fog. You are probably having a few negative thoughts while reading this so far right now! That is ok. **Once you realize and acknowledge your depression, anxiety, PTSD, or overall mental struggles, then you know you are going to have to change.**

Your first step is to interrupt your negative thoughts and emotions with positive thoughts, words, and affirmations.

In this next section, I don't want to just tell you what to do, but I want you to know my experience as well. If I did not exist, these nine principles you need to have in your schedule are still relevant. It does not matter if I write this book or not; these principles are universal outside of my experience. My goal is to encourage you and let you know that you are not alone. If I can do it, then you can do it too!

Set and Keep a Consistent Schedule

Consistency is key. Having a consistent schedule will allow for more structure throughout your day. It will keep you focused with maintaining the proper intentions to have a constructive day. It also allows you to have more flexibility in handling your tasks and goals that you are shooting for. There are so many tools that you can use to keep up with a consistent schedule. Your smart phone, a daily planner, or just write it down on a Post-it Note. Either way, you have to start somewhere. Your daily plan and routine starts the night before. It should be written out in your planner or in your phone, and you will review it before you go to sleep. That is how you will be intentional about your day. **Be excited about tomorrow when reading your plan today!**

Here are nine action steps of what you need to have in your calendar planned for every day:

1) Wake up/sleep time
2) 10 minutes prayer/meditation/affirmations
3) Meals/snacks
4) Water intake
5) Positive self-grooming

6) Exercise/movement routine

7) Society contribution (work, studies, volunteering)

8) 30 minutes of self-development

9) 5-minute phone call/face conversation

Fewer than ten action steps that you are going to be deliberate about daily. If you pay close attention, at least six of the steps you already do every day, so you should not feel overwhelmed. All you are doing is focusing on them to ensure you are as intentional in your daily living as possible. Repetition is the mother of all skill.

1) *Wake Up/ Sleep Time*

Be committed to wake up at least thirty to sixty minutes before you currently wake up, regardless of your level of responsibilities. I am talking to you if you are married with kids, if you have pets, or are currently by yourself or single. It does not matter. Along with an earlier wake-up time, you should be setting a good bedtime for yourself. There are two parts to this equation. Rest is extremely important in your fight for your mental health. So, scheduling to factor in at least six hours of sleep is crucial. This new push includes establishing creative boundaries and rules for yourself.

Get up IMMEDIATELY!!! No more hitting the snooze button multiple times a morning. No scrolling on social media. No hanging out. Just get up! Having the "spring in your step" first thing in the morning sets the precedent for the rest of the day. I know there are going to be days that you will absolutely not want to get out of the bed or start your day. It is accumulating the small wins in your day that adds up over time. Having the days that you jump out of bed and get your day started on the best foot are the days that you can possibly have your best days.

My most significant change happened when I made the decision to start getting up at a set time every day. I decided that I was not going to lay around in bed anymore. I was going to spearhead the mornings with Steph and the kids. I had always been on a set schedule and routine since I could remember, until my diagnosis and subsequent symptoms took over my life. That is what allowed me to focus on the tasks at hand and accomplish daily goals I set for myself.

The amount of caffeine and sugar that is consumed in a day has a direct impact on your quality of sleep. That includes alcohol. Your blood sugar changes when you are consuming alcoholic beverages. When you are drinking right before bed, you may notice that you wake up in the middle of the night. A lot of times, it has to do with the fact that your blood sugar level just crashes and it screws your body up. Just say your normal bedtime is around 9-10 p.m. (and if it is not, then change it). You should not have any caffeinated beverages, products, or supplements past 1 p.m. That lasting effect of the caffeine can have a direct impact on your ability to go to sleep and, most importantly, stay asleep. So be mindful of the caffeinated teas, coffee, energy drinks, alcohol, high sugar content drinks, anything of the sort that you have late at night.

Some people may be wondering why they cannot sleep, and they have to take these different sleep aids to assist them, but when you do that, you may not realize you may be prolonging the problem. If you don't know these things already, then you don't know why you cannot figure out your sleep issues.

It is recommended to get at least seven to nine hours of sleep every night. EVERY NIGHT.[5]

I was only getting two, three, sometimes four hours of sleep a night. Six hours was a dream night for me. I would be up all night and attempt to function for an entire day the

---

[5] "How Much Sleep Do We Really Need: Revisited," National Sleep Foundation, https://www.sleepfoundation.org/articles/how-much-sleep-do-we-really-need

next day. That took a serious toll on my mind, body, and spirit. When I made the commitment to sleep consistently by turning off my television and electronic devices, that's when I began to feel a physical shift within that helped me get my life back on track. By turning off my TV and phone every night, it made me focus on my breathing and heartbeat, thoughts and emotions. It may sound corny, but it helped a ton! I did not have the distractions of the outside world dominating my psyche right before I fell asleep. I was able to steer and control my mind in a positive direction.

2) *Ten Minutes Prayer/Meditation/Affirmations*

Take your time to pray, meditate, get lost in some good music, or find a quiet place to allow your mind freedom. Give yourself permission to daydream or envision where you want to be and where your life will be. **What determines your thinking will determine your life.** Whether it's God or your maker, take that time to center yourself and relax. Now, combining these three things can help you to gain clarity and perspective in your life. It might not feel effective overnight nor in the first week or the early months. But just like anything in life, you need to practice. And if you want it that bad, you will do it.

Everyone has something to be grateful for. If you are reading this book, your literacy is something to be grateful for. If you are holding this book, your functioning hands and fingers are something to be grateful for. Start with three things right now that you are grateful for.

1) _____

2) _____

3) _____

Take a moment and ask yourself when was the last time that you thanked your feet for getting you places and back home? Or the last time you were thankful to pick up a spoon or fork to scoop your food to bring to your mouth? Even the last time the left side of your brain thanked the right side or vice versa?

I start my gratitude from the second I wake up. Three things right then and there. I am grateful for waking up, first of all. Second, I have breath in my lungs and, third, the brain and muscle function for my feet to touch the ground. I am starting out my day positive, and I am technically in bed! Combining these three things helped me to gain clarity and perspective in my life since I was so far off for so long.

3) *Meals/Snacks*

How you fuel yourself will determine how you feel. If you are eating junk, and you feel like junk, that is just going to perpetuate a problem. The fuel you put into your body is the equivalent to the proper fuel that you put in a race car. If you treat it like a Pinto, it will perform like a Pinto. But if you treat it like a Formula 1 race car, then that is the performance you should expect!

If you start to fuel your body with some good and healthy nutrients, then it is going to start to have an impact on your overall health. It may not change the way you feel right away, but there will be small, impactful changes to your overall internal health.

Health Tip One: Incorporate green, leafy vegetables into your diet every day. Not just eating a salad by itself, but having broccoli, brussels sprouts, asparagus, green beans, etc., with your protein and carbohydrates. All of the things we could not wait to have as kids!

Health Tip Two: Have good, healthy protein that is not too fatty. If you can make the health-conscious choice of protein without the skin or not fried, choose the baked option or non-fried option.

Health Tip Three: Incorporate healthy carbs when possible. Science has consistently dubbed carbs as your brain's food. French fries and potato chips are not a good regular part of a diet. Substitute raw or low-sodium nuts for the junk snacks. Fruit in moderation is also a great source of healthy carbs, but no fruit juices.

Health Tip Four: Consume a balance of protein, carbs, and veggies mixed with fruit and healthy snacks in your daily diet. Make sure you are eating frequent small meals as well and not just snacking on junk food throughout your day. Portion control is a big reason why people are not in the healthiest of shapes in life. They say they are eating protein, carbs, and veggies; however, they are completely off in the portion sizes that are consumed. Just a rule of thumb to follow for serving sizes and for men, it is double measurements:

- Proteins- the size of your palm
- Carbs- cupped hand
- Veggies- fist size[6]

---

[6] Mary Jane, "9 Tips to Measure and Control Portion Sizes," 19 November 2018 https://www.healthline.com/nutrition/portion-control#section3

Next time you serve yourself, ask if this is what your plate looks like. If not, make the proper adjustments to get on track! By eating every three to four hours, your body will not go through the overstuffed then starving cycle that people tend to eat like. You want your body energy to be as even as possible. **Your gut health has a direct impact on your mental health.**

You will want to seek guidance from your health professional in regard to embarking on a fast or a cleanse to clean out your system. An annual fast or a three to five day cleanse may be exactly what your body needs to make a reset.

When I got away from my normal eating habits is when I started to feel the most sluggish, I had ever felt. My clothes did not fit like before. I was not moving as fast as I used to. I was always going to the bathroom because all of these things fast food will do to you. It was pizza, burgers, pasta, fried chicken, etc. No vegetables in sight. When I got to my heaviest weight ever, that's when I made the decision to recommit to my healthy eating lifestyle as before. My body started to thank me immediately!

Fuel your body. Fuel your mind. Fuel your soul.

4) *Water Intake*

When I say hydrate, I am talking about one resource only. Water. Up to 60 percent of our body is made up of water. It is the single most abundant nutrient in the human body.[7]

Some people do not realize that drinking tea, coffee, and energy drinks actually deplete your hydration levels. Sodas, juice, carbonated beverages, and sports drinks all dehydrate you. If you drink caffeinated drinks on a daily basis, reflect on cutting back on occasion. This will do wonders for your body as well as your wallet! Be prepared for the with-drawl effects, though. Headaches, irritability, fatigue, and just being plain old mean are some symptoms when weaning off sugars and caffeine. These are very real addictions that people battle with, and just remember, we are making small changes to result in huge wins over time.

Water is extremely important because it keeps your vital organs hydrated and working properly. It also flushes out toxins from your system while carrying nutrients to cells. Water can also increase your metabolism by up to 20 percent, depending on how much you drink per day. It gives your body form and structure. Did you know it is a

---

[7] "The Water in You: Water and the Human Body," U.S. Geological Survey https://www.usgs.gov/special-topic/water-science-school/science/water-you-water-and-human-body?qt-science_center_objects=0#qt-science_center_objects

natural appetite suppressor and helps with metabolizing stored fat in your body? These are some very important things water does for us.

Today, the National Academy of Medicine recommends letting thirst guide your water consumption habits but that you set an even higher volume of total daily water intake: 3.7 liters (15 cups) for the average adult male and 2.7 liters (11 cups) for the average adult female.[8]

5) *Positive Self-Grooming*

"You look good, you feel good." There is so much truth to that statement. Every time you wash your hands in the bathroom, you see yourself in the mirror. Every time you pass a reflection, you are going to see yourself. One of the first things you can do to get into a better state of mind has to do with the little things. Taking care of yourself should be a part of your regular routine. It may seem like a statement that is obvious, but it is not that simple for people. Being deliberate on getting up and preparing for the day by brushing your teeth, taking a shower, and

---

[8] "Do I really need to drink 8 glasses of water a day?" One Medical, https://www.onemedical.com/blog/live-well/daily-water-intake/

combing your hair is a crucial step in the process of positive actions.

Having the confidence in yourself for the day is part of your self-grooming. Lying around in your pajamas or sweats, you have a tendency to feel and stay in that funk you are in. It is all about looking the part.

This is not about pleasing others. It is really about tapping into treating yourself right and how you and your body deserve to be treated. This is not a vain piece of advice. This is not about being a magazine cover model. It is about feeling good from the inside out and being proud of yourself. These are the things that will help pull you out, even though they may sound like they won't! You have to remember, if this is a part of your routine that you have lost, then this is something you really have to do the extra work to step back into.

I remember the days when Steph would ask me if I had taken a shower and it would have been several days that had passed. My beard was growing longer by the second. My hair was more disheveled than the day prior, and I could start to feel a film on my teeth. As a man, the personal self-grooming that should happen daily is washing my face, brushing and flossing my teeth, combing my hair, putting on deodorant after a shower, and shaving.

When I started to make sure that part of my routine was daily hygiene maintenance, I felt tremendously better. Even though I had nowhere to go! To know that I put a brush to my hair, brushed my teeth, and washed my face while putting on something presentable to wear helped me begin to look at myself a little bit differently.

Because I looked at myself differently, I felt different. When I felt different, then I felt like I could do more.

**How you present yourself to
yourself is important!**

6) *Exercise/Movement Routine*

Move your body! Whether it is going to your local gym, boot camp, yoga, etc. Or going for a walk around the block or climbing the stairs instead of the escalator or elevator. Whatever it is, go and move your body.

If the best you can give is walking to the corner of your block and back, that is AWESOME! Make it happen. For others, maybe all you do is train. Maybe now what you do is change up *how* you train. If all you do is cardio, try Pilates or yoga. If your routine is HIIT or strength exclusively, give another form of cardio a go for a change. Just begin to open up your mind to doing something a little different. That is the most important part. You need to start breaking those old patterns and incorporating new positive ones if you are in a certain routine. If you feel like you have this section in a healthy place in your life, then kudos to you!

Your comfort zone can be both a gift and a curse. People build their lives to be as comfortable as possible; however, that is such a detrimental place to be if you are trying to improve your mental state and get better. You need to trick your brain. You need to shock your body. You have to keep your spirit alive by feeding it more of a positive environment as often as possible. **There are so many beautiful places if you pick your chin up and do something radically new in life!** It all starts with taking one step outside your door. Then another. Then another.

Bodies are built for movement. It promotes overall health both physically and mentally, which, in turn, reduces stress and anxiety levels. If you need a helping hand to not be alone in this process, find the person who is always there for you and ask for help.

By getting out of my comfort zone and putting myself in a different environment, it changes the structure of the thoughts in my mind. It allows me to think differently. Some days, walking to the mailbox was a huge win for me.

Those were millimeter days. Other days, I took the kids to the park or to ride bikes outside. Those were days I felt like I moved two feet. I don't mean feet or millimeters literally, but that was the way I was measuring progress in my mind. It was not an easy process for me whatsoever. I was intentional and deliberate in making myself move. At first, it did not happen daily; however, when I did have a day when I was moving my body, I felt a significant difference in my attitude and overall demeanor.

7) *Society Contribution*

Listen. You need to be good citizens. Period. To your neighbor and neighborhood. To your cities. To your counties. To your states and ultimately to your country. It is your duty to push yourself to achieve more in life whether that is in your job, in your education, or in your personal life with volunteering and helping others. It is extremely important for you to find an opportunity to better yourself by getting promoted within your current job position, or if starting your own business is a passion, then do it. If you have not finished schooling or want to achieve higher education, then do it. Find an opportunity to help others in need with no expectation of returns. Go out there and work hard. For yourself or others. We all have an obligation to do better and be more for each other and, most importantly, ourselves.

I can say that I am in a place now that's much better than where I was before, but I am not even close to the person I know I can become. One of the reasons why I am improving more daily is by focusing on others and not myself.

It was through opportunities that I was presented with when I was starting to climb out of my hole of depression, anxiety, stress, and PTSD that I got to see the light at the end of the tunnel. It may sound like a redundant subject in regard to giving, but it was worth a try for me. It is not only about material giving, either. Birthday presents, holidays, and anniversaries are times when gifts and giving are always assumed. I am referring to more than the expectations. **When I started to give my time, energy, and emotions to others, I felt the true nature of gratitude.**

8) *Thirty Minutes of Self-Development*

This is really about taking the time to utilize tools that will make you stronger mentally. Based on your goal, it will behoove you to find somebody who has already accomplished what you are looking to do and use their tips and strategies. That is considered mentorship. That is just one piece to developing yourself. Books are a huge aspect in the development phase. The library is one the best and least expensive resources for you to hack getting to your personal goals faster. Not having to take the time learning things the hard way when you can use tools and strategies from others is a big deal with compressing time frames.

There are so many free resources that are available to use via the internet and social media as well. You really have to pinpoint what you are looking to accomplish in life and study up as much as you can.

Remember, though: knowledge without action is a total waste. If you do not take action on your development, then what is the point of it all?

Beyond mentors, you can use counselors or therapists to provide you with unbiased feedback. The whole purpose is to grow. You will need to develop:

The ability to overcome challenges by using resources available.

Being open to hear a different perspective from someone else.

Your knowledge base about the current events of your diagnosis by learning, studying, and growing.

The ability to identify what those areas of biggest opportunities to grow are in all areas to challenge yourself to grow and develop into a better version of yourself.

You have to work on you!

9) *Five Minute Phone Call/Face Conversation*

This action is going to take you from the isolation zone as you have to get out of the comfort zone and be intentional and make connections again. It may be calling Grandma for five minutes every day. She may feel like she is the special one because you are checking in on her, but really, it is you making the effort to connect. It could be a parent, child, or best friend. Whomever. Either a phone call or an actual face-to-face interaction, which is ideal.

Jaime Wiebe gives five ways to strengthen your support system:

1) Know what you want from a support system
2) Build your bonds with existing family and friends
3) Embrace your interests
4) Expand your professional connections

5) Create your own personal support area[9]

The goal of the call is that you need a strengthened support system, but your first step could just be the phone call. You are going to need relationships to make it through this journey, but just start with a call. If you are feeling comfortable to share how you are doing, then share. Start with the intention of asking them about their day, their positive parts of life, etc. Just start to get into the routine.

When I started to integrate this into my daily routine, I honestly had to go back to the basics of being social again. It sounds so trivial to some, but to me, I felt like I regressed years. I was so wrapped up in my mind, thoughts, and emotions I had zero room for anyone who I loved. I was getting back what I was giving out, which was not much at all. However, little by little, I began to climb out of that hole I felt trapped in.

Then I started to be present again at family gatherings, parties, and places like that. There were days that I spent all day with my family and friends outside of my comfort zone, aka my house. Do not get me wrong; within an hour or so, I would find my quiet corner and zone out. But I was

---

[9] Jamie Wiebe, "5 Ways to Strengthen Your Support System," 10 April 2019, https://www.talkspace.com/blog/how-to-strengthen-your-support-system/

physically present. Those days were full of anxiety, stress, fun, uncertainty, and a whole gamut of emotions. I HAD TO DO IT. Eventually, I WANTED TO. **The question is, what moves you, a must or a want?** I knew I WANTED to, and I MUST. I decided to do more every day and eventually started to see a brighter light for my future.

The work with my family began to pay dividends. Stephanie and I became much stronger in our bond. Even though I was working on *myself,* stability began to come back in life with my kids and her. There were plenty of moments that I still did not feel complete; however, I began to notice my hard work was paying off in my household.

Build Your Community

You cannot nor are you supposed to do life alone. Some people do not have their natural family or the one they were born into. Everyone should have that one person in their life whether it be a mother/father figure, or someone like a brother or sister or actual siblings that you can connect with in that family bond. Having some of that family time is very important. Some people have to replace that with friends, and that is ok too. Making sure to create time in your schedule to spend time connecting with them, being with them, or doing life with them is critical to building your community.

The other important area is your faith or ideology. Whatever your belief system may be, it is important to share community with those who have your similar beliefs because that will reaffirm your foundational experiences. It will bring you back to your core of who you are as a person and what that belief system that surrounds you can provide to you in a community setting.

The third source of community is the mental wellness community. Maybe it's your small group that you attend that's specifically designated to address your mental diagnosis. It may be your therapist who you see on a weekly or monthly basis. Really making sure that you are in a community setting or have your community intact will help you to continue to address directly what you are facing with your mental wellness.

This is a journey, and just like exercising your body, you also need to exercise your mental health. Everyone has a brain and everybody that is able to be blessed enough to get up, walk, talk, have a conscience, and be able to do things for themselves all face different issues. Those who are at their lowest point or suffering at the moment really need to make having this specific area of community as a part of the plan and routine.

If you are in the thick of it right now, with the feeling of just barely treading water or have the thoughts of not wanting to talk to anyone let alone be around family and experiencing denial on all levels, it is going to be ok.

- 43.3 percent of U.S. adults with mental illness received treatment in 2018.

- 64.1 percent of U.S. adults with serious mental illness received treatment in 2018.

- 50.6 percent of U.S. youth aged 6-17 with a mental health disorder received treatment in 2016.

- The average delay between onset of mental illness symptoms and treatment is eleven years.[10]

If your community is disconnecting from you, it may be because you are disconnecting from them. You have to make the effort to reconnect with those who have loved you and supported you unconditionally and have reached out to

---

[10] "Mental Health by the Numbers," National Alliance on Mental Illness, September 2019, https://www.nami.org/learn-more/mental-health-by-the-numbers

you. You have to acknowledge within yourself that if those connections are now severed, it is probably you unplugging. **It is never too late to reconnect!**

If you know someone or it is you that is dealing with a challenging diagnosis, you have to lean in on your support system. If you do not feel supported by friends and loved ones, utilize the professional resources that are available to you. Remember the statistics I wrote about earlier? Never feel like you are alone in what you are experiencing. Not all incidents are alike; however, symptoms may be the same and so can treatments. Try to use who you have closest to you first. Friends, family, co-workers, pastors/ priests, shared groups, etc. The possibilities are endless.

GET HELP

The best way to get help is to conduct the best research. Go to positive sources as opposed to just going by other peoples' experiences alone. There is also a need to have scientific knowledge about the diagnosis specific to the individuals seeking understanding.

If you are reading this book and have gotten this far and you are saying to yourself, "I do not want to feel this way any longer than I have to," this step is the most important to what you need to do. If you are the kind of person who does not accept help, you need to change that. Most people are afraid to recognize knowledge, but that needs to change as well.

STEP ONE: Admit You Need Help

When I looked Stephanie in her eyes and uttered those three words, "I need help," she came to life in a way I had never seen before. It was like she had a brand-new sense of purpose. I have loved her for many years, and in this instance, I witnessed her strength and absolute love for me. Never, ever underestimate the power and strength of the person you have standing directly next to you. She set up my appointments. She made sure I got to and from where I needed to be because she truly understood the severity. When I finally told her I needed to talk to somebody, I didn't want to know that something was wrong with me.

While I felt fragile psychologically, I felt strong physically. Because of the physical demands of being a firefighter, I was in the best shape of my life. I have faced bodily injury in my personal life and during my time as a firefighter, which I can point to and say, "It hurts." You break a bone in your body, you splint or cast it, and in a few weeks, it should be healed, right? Acknowledging a mental trauma, however, was more challenging for me. I could not just point and say, "It hurts here."

When I finally told Steph, "I need help," those three words were the three most difficult, and yet liberating, words that I had ever spoken. I knew I could either continue down my current path and be a hero to everyone else or change my direction and become a hero to myself, my wife, and my kids.

When it comes to finding the proper help that you deserve, it is going to take some time and a little homework. You are going to need to figure out what area in your life you need help with in the first place then move in that direction to identify the resources you need. You have to acknowledge that you need the help first and foremost. That will be the most important part of your whole journey. It is imperative for you to find the right kind of help also. This is not an automatic plug that everyone fits into and it happens to work. If what you are trying is not working for you, pivot, find a new direction, and try again.

- **Get your facts straight.** That is going to require you to do a bit of reading. If your views about psychologists and psychiatrists are that they are quacks, if you think group therapy is for sissys, or if your thoughts are all negative around how to regain your mental wellness and strength, you are going to take the long, bumpy, painful road. But because you answered yes to the first step of PUSH, I know you are capable and are willing to start opening up your mind to getting your facts straight and learning about what you are experiencing from a research standpoint and getting help by gaining knowledge. The more you put into it, the more you are going to grow, get stronger, have a better understanding, and have sharper tools to PUSH, to combat, and to work through this.

- **Focus on every step before you cross the finish line.** *For many people, it is the start that stops them.* Read that again. It is not an easy task to admit something is not right with how you may be feeling emotionally, physically, or mentally. It is human nature to protect yourself. When you finally admit to yourself that you need help, that's one thing. It is a whole different monster to say it to someone else out loud. When you do, though, it could feel like a two-ton boulder lifted off your shoulders. Sometimes the scariest actions result in the most favorable outcomes.

- **Recognize you are powerless in this.** Just as in AA when referencing addictions, you have go to something bigger than yourself. That is why you can go to the group for help and accountability. You can seek God in a spiritual sense. If it is the universe or a different type of spiritual for you, then seek that also. But you have to go beyond yourself because this is a monster that you have never faced before, while others have and are overcoming on a daily basis.

The hard way is trying to do this alone. White knuckling this is just not dealing with this challenge in a productive way. Not reaching out for help, not changing.

When you want something...see it the way it really is. See it the way you want it to be. Make it the way you want it to be.

Step Two: Swap Unhealthy Pushes for Healthy Pushes

There are seemingly unlimited ways to reach the same destinations in life. Some paths are good and some are bad. In your journey of mental health and wellness, you want to take the paths that are going to be the most beneficial for you. There may be a few areas that you feel like you are doing the right thing in; however, they can actually be detrimental to your overall health.

Unhealthy Push Number One: **Assume other people grasp your struggles.** You are on a mental health journey that is a daily battle to win and manage your thoughts, feelings, and emotions. You do not want to fall into the trap of thinking that everyone is going to understand. This goes back into reconnecting with those who you may have lost touch with. Just because you ask for help and people now hear and know what your challenges are, do not assume it is going to change for them and now they get what you are going through. It does not mean that they understand; they just now know what you are going through. That is it. There is a distinct difference between "understanding" and "knowing what you are going through". Knowing what you are going through means now people have a name for your actions. PTSD, anxiety, depression etc.

To *understand* however, people need to have that personal experience to tie it back to. "I understand the stress and depression that you are going through because I had similar challenges in my life" is what puts it in a different perspective for others. That can be a positive when people understand you because of their shared types of experiences. You want to avoid the assumption because it can put you right back into the anger, resentment, and isolation phase that you are leaving behind. That pitfall can deter the step of reconnecting and engaging with family and friends, and they probably have no idea they did anything wrong.

It is not for them to understand; it is for you to get more comfortable in talking about your challenges!

Healthy Push: Take the time to share a little more about your experiences and what you are going through. Help them to understand what you are experiencing so they have a better opportunity to process these new feelings and ask questions or educate themselves on the importance of your new challenges. Having a few conversations with the right people will allow you to be more comfortable in talking through your thoughts, feelings, and emotions.

Unhealthy Push Number Two: **Changing everything at once.** There are possibly parts of your life that are going well and parts that are not. If you change everything at once trying to get back on track, it has the potential of being overwhelming, which will lead to a constant spiral out of control. If you decide to switch up everything, then you will not be able to measure your progress in the areas that are your strengths as opposed to your weaknesses. If you stop or miss out on one of your new changes, then it may become a snowball effect for the rest of the things you want to change. Since you did not wake up early as planned, then you cannot accomplish the other tasks you wanted to for the day. Then you are right back to square one.

Healthy Push: Take one section of life that needs to be improved. Make small, incremental changes every day, and you can adjust to what is going well compared to what you may need to shift or tweak to suit your needs. These are small-scale changes on a daily basis, which can and will result in major effects over time. When you have built a bit of confidence, then add another part of life to strengthen and focus on that as well. Do not feel like these changes will take forever. Many people make changes and experience results in days and weeks!

Unhealthy Push Number Three: **Assuming that with major progress you may be seeing and feeling, that you are "cured" or everything is "all good now."** "I do not have to do any more" is a HUGE red flag to managing your mental health every day. It is something that is a constant fight for people. When you think that you are good to go, then you will stop doing the small, basic things that are keeping you on the right track in the first place. You will notice that when you start slipping, you can easily look back and realize what you are now letting slide and not keeping up with. You will know the one or two parts of your day you absolutely have to stay on top of in order to have a winning day! If you miss a few days of your movement routine, then other parts of your day have the potential to start to fall to the wayside.

Healthy Push: Attack your day with the same amount of drive and tenacity as you can for yourself. Treat it as the first day of a new beginning. Be very deliberate in your actions, and do not allow yourself to be compromised for any reason other than success. Keep laser focused on your tasks at hand and push like your life depends on it. If you do slip up, do not beat yourself up over it. Take a pause, take a deep breath, figure out how you can shift, then keep moving.

Unhealthy Push Number Four: **Altering your state**. If it is not doctor-prescribed and you can avoid altering your mind with drugs or alcohol to escape your present feelings and push them off until later to deal with anyway, then avoid it. That has the potential to get you relaxed and comfortable while going through these changes in life. **You need to have clarity of mind.** These substances take you to a place. You think you feel good, but really it is a depressant that is taking you further down a hole and you do not realize that at the moment. That is a huge pitfall that people fall into over and over and over. They cannot understand why they still have the same problems the next day when they should have looked at how much they were escaping the present with drugs and alcohol.

Healthy Push: Evaluate how much time and effort it takes from your life to consume alcohol and/or drugs for escaping and replace that time with healthy alternatives. You may not realize how much time you may be able to free up by skipping the drugs and alcohol. Time is the most precious commodity on this planet, and any amount you can unchain is more precious than you may think. Fill that time with healthy, positive, uplifting interests and further your self-development.

Remember, it is not for them. This is all for you and your journey!

Step Three: Recognize Your Wins and Celebrate!

When utilizing all of these steps every day and seeing that you succeeded in beating your emotions and were successful in having a great day, it is most important to recognize this and celebrate. Society doesn't celebrate enough wins, and yet people harp on losses all of the time. You don't have to take a first-class, five-star trip just because you made it out of bed before noon. You can reward yourself with little things consistently, and then you establish an attitude of positive rewarding, not negative self-talk. Set a goal and have the reward attached to it. Make sure your reward is equivalent to your goal. When you accomplish what you set for yourself, then bust out the streamers! If you do not hit it, however, do not beat yourself up over it. Use that time to reevaluate what could go better next time, pivot, and do it again. Do not reward yourself anyway. That will have negative effects on the whole point of rewarding yourself for doing well. It's time to shift your mind, move your body, adjust your emotions, and start winning every single day. You don't win just one game and expect to win the championship. It's consistent wins over and over and over that will get you to where you envision your life to be.

You need to be open to something new. When you are pushing, you are doing something new, creating goals, becoming intentional, and winning in life again. Set up a plan for your day. EVERY DAY.

PUSH is broken down into simple steps that are clearly defined so you do not have to put any guesswork into it. Getting out of your comfort zone/doing something new allows you to have more clarity on what kind of plan to make and what steps you need to take to get better. By setting and keeping a consistent schedule, it ensures you are as intentional in your daily living as possible. When you build your community, it establishes your sense of connection with those you love and care for.

Admitting that you need to get help cannot be overstated. There is no getting better without this step here. Once you have come to grips with the need for help, that is when the real work starts. You have to apply your life to the steps. Choose what you can apply to your life in whatever area you are already not implementing. You may have to adopt a whole new set of daily habits and coping mechanisms, or you may just be implementing a few steps to make your current system better, depending on where you are at.

Your life has a purpose. Your story is important. Your dreams count.

Your voice matters. You were born to make an impact.

STEP TWO: TOWARD
Establish a Plan + Take Steps

Moving in a specific and deliberate direction with a goal in mind is what toward means. **Your life should be driven by your vision, your mission, your direction, and whatever it is in your gut and soul that just burns and yearns to be better.** You cannot get anywhere directionally without an aim. You need something to push toward.

Vision is the art of seeing what is invisible to others.
- Jonathan Swift -

You are PUSHING, which means you are getting out of your comfort zone and doing something new. That is giving your mind freedom to explore new ideas and opportunities that are there for you. You are having challenging thoughts, feelings, and emotions that you would not have even imagined before. You are setting and keeping a consistent schedule, which is allowing you to tackle small goals and tasks that have always been a desire for you to attain. Constantly achieving small victories daily is giving you new insight on the possibilities of a new and brighter future. You are building your community and reconnecting with people you have been wanting to as well as building new relationships because you are out of your comfort zone. That is allowing you to find new resources to help you in your everyday journey to be a better person. Now you are finally getting the help you deserve since you made the first step in acknowledging what you needed.

Now you are in the stage of TOWARD, which is directional. You are advancing toward your goals with intent and laser focus. It does not matter what the goal may be. It can be as simple as being a better husband/wife. It can consist of wanting to take the biggest leap of your life and build a business or run for a huge promotion. It can be as simple as waking up to an alarm clock with good intentions on crushing your day. Whatever it is, you need to know which direction to point to and run, crawl, walk, or sprint to it as long as you are moving in the right direction with the right intentions.

TOWARD - in the direction of getting closer to achieving (a goal), close or closer to[11]

Answer these questions as clearly and honestly as possible.

- Who and/or what do you want to become?

- Where do you want to go?

- Where are you and where do you want to be?

- What's your why?

If these questions are too much for you right now, it is ok, I understand! Finish reading this chapter and come back to these for a better idea on how to answer them. If you cannot figure them out, ask other people who are close to you—since you are building your community and reconnecting—how they see you!

Here are the steps you are going to focus on in this phase of your journey:

1) Establish your goal

---

[11]"Toward," Dictionary.com, Accessed 16 May 2020, https://www.dictionary.com/browse/toward?s=t

2) Action steps to achieve your goal

3) Measure your progress

4) Re-evaluate yourself

You do not need to feel overwhelmed by trying to change everything and have a bunch of new goals at once. Pick one. Concentrate on accomplishing that first. **As you reach your goals, you will then start to incorporate new and bigger goals!**

How to Establish Your Goal

Goal- the result or achievement toward which effort is directed; aim; end.[12]

I remember what the very first goal that I had in my mind was, though I did not call it a goal at the time but a strong and raw feeling I had. I definitely was not in the state of mind to start establishing goals. It was to make sure I re-established a relationship with Stephanie and our two kids. I could not lose them from my life.

---

[12]"Goal," Dictionary.com, Accessed 16 May 2020, https://www.dictionary.com/browse/goal?s=t

I honestly did not have a plan. Don't be fooled and think I had a sit down, write it all out strategy session because that was the farthest from the truth. I was doing what I felt was best at the exact moment that I was making these kinds of decisions. It was purely a reactive approach as opposed to a defensive strategy. I am hopeful that this can give you a bit of insight about how important it is to stay ahead of this as much as possible. I did not, and it had a huge impact on our life.

As a result, I had to navigate some very muddy waters to figure out what changes I needed to make in order for that to happen. At the same time, I knew I did not have an automatic say so in what was going to change. I could not tell the kids that they were just going to be good and they were going to love me and love being around me. It was daily steps, process, and interactions that I had to make to gain a little of their trust every day before they could trust that if they did something wrong, or not, that they would not get yelled at anymore. Or if they made a mistake, acted up, or cried, whatever toddlers do, that they were not going to feel scared because of it.

That was my goal. It was not career focused anymore. It was now family, relationship, and love focused. I have since been told that I have accomplished the goal of rebuilding my family in an amazing way. My relationship with my extended family has been repaired. My relationship with my wife Stephanie and our kids has been repaired. It started from a simple change in focus. In order to fix what I had broken, I had to make it a priority to fix.

It required me to take time and figure out how to be a father and a husband again. It took a couple of years for all four of us to navigate through together. I had to go through my own process of figuring out what family meant to me and what I was willing to do to make it right.

Goals are imperative in living life to your fullest potential. They do not have to be tangible or materialistic. The goals that you can't see or touch somehow become the most important goals in people's lives. Everyone has goals in life. You might not recognize it as a goal, though. It may be a feeling, emotion, or thought in your mind that is unwavering. Either way, you can and must work on achieving those things for your life.

Goals need to have certain elements to be effective. An effective goal:

- is clearly defined
- has a time frame clearly associated with it

- you define what the achievement looks like
- is measurable

You need to know that your goal, whatever you are pushing toward, can be tangible or intangible. Toward is the goal, what you want to accomplish. What is one thing that right now you may think is nearly impossible to do?

- Going out on a date with your significant other?
- Being present in a public place?
- Getting into great physical shape?
- Waking up and not feel crushed before the day even starts?
- Learning a new language, playing an instrument?
- Reconnect with people who you love?
- Getting better sleep at night?
- Being on time?

Getting around larger group settings is close to impossible for some. I am talking about a room full of ten family members. That is how bad it can be. Those feelings are all so real to so many people. It may feel like you are the only one who thinks like that and who understands that, or maybe it feels or sounds kind of crazy to yourself. *Who doesn't want to hang out with their friends or family? I cannot say that out loud! I don't want to hang out or talk or please do not call me.* These are very real types of feelings for people.

Goals. There's no telling what you can do when you get inspired by them. There's no telling what you can do when you believe in them. And there's no telling what will happen when you act upon them.

- Jim Rohn -

Just know if you pick one, two, or all of those previous points, you are not alone. Plug in your own goals right here.

1) _____

2) _____

3) _____

4) _____

How did that make you feel just writing it? Scared? Overwhelmed? Terrified? Intimidated? Good for all of those feelings. You can easily turn them to excited, thrilled, overjoyed, jubilant. You can and will be able to work through it. Your goal can be very simple. It does not have to be some big project. It can be as straightforward as getting out of bed and becoming productive toward whatever tasks you need to handle for the day.

Action Steps to Achieve Your Goal

Goals that do not have action driving them are merely ideas and good intentions. You need to have clearly defined action steps that you can look at and realize immediately if you are on track or if you need to alter your course. There needs to be a conscious, deliberate intention behind what you are doing.

For example, if a goal of yours is about reconnecting with loved ones, a few action steps you can implement could be:

- I will ensure that I am not taking things to heart with my friends and family by making sure I see the positive and smile more often.

- I will make sure that my family and friends know and feel that I love them by the hugs, kisses, and positive words that I now speak over them.

- I will be conscious of the words and responses that I have for people regardless of what mood I am in.

If you are looking to progress in your education, start a new business venture, or run for a promotion, how are you going to break down a huge accomplishment into manageable chunks? They do not have to be long and drawn out either. As a matter of fact, the simpler they are, the better! **You should always operate with a strategy and action steps.**

Measure Your Progress

The entire reason for measuring your progress is to determine how well you are doing and determine if any adjustments need to be made. When you are looking to measure yourself, keep it simple. Are you closer to achieving your goal today than last week? Great! What did you do that allowed you to move in the right direction and achieve progress, no matter how little it may seem? For instance, if your goal is to learn a new language, can you recite and define ten words this week and it was six words last week? That is huge progress. If you are writing a book and you have a few hundred more words this month compared to last month, then that is progress. See how simple it is? Now you want to ensure you are measuring within your set time frame as well. **It is much easier and you feel better for rewarding yourself for something good as opposed to beating yourself up for something bad.**

Consistency is also key with measuring your progress. How consistent were you this week compared to last week? Did you set a goal to work out five times this week but only hit three days while last week you made it to all five days? If you are consistent more often than not, that is progress. Ultimately, this will lead you into a consistent routine, which is the ultimate goal. **When you have the consistent routine and schedule established, then you start to hit your goals and get some wins under your belt.** If you can stay consistent, then you will be able to measure your progress much easier and it becomes second nature for you.

Re-Evaluate Yourself

You are going to ensure you are still moving in the same direction by constantly re-evaluating your movements. It is kind of like putting yourself on probation at a new job. They typically have a 90- to 120-day window for employees to determine if they want to keep you or let you go. With that being said, some jobs have sit-downs every thirty days to perform an update, especially if it is not going so well. They want to try and give you an opportunity to make some corrections and get on board. You can do the same with yourself, except with a little grace. You have to give yourself that room to say this process is not going to be perfect and you may not hit the mark the first few times. It may be hit and miss, and it surely is not going to be awesome every day! It is ok, though. As long as you are pushing forward toward your goal. Every fifteen to thirty days, check in with yourself. This is an honest evaluation to ensure you are on the right track and feel good about your progress. It is not a negative exercise. Look at it through positive eyes!

In some instances, you may have to re-evaluate your goals as well. Sometimes your goals may change because you are not the same person who set the goals up in the first place. If you find yourself in this predicament, make the necessary changes and alter your course. It is ok to pivot out of certain situations that you may not have as much drive in as before. Better to do that than keep plodding along just because. It is important to have a goal in life because without it, you lack direction. When you lack direction, you feel more lost. Call it your vision, your goal, your mission, your direction, whatever you want. Just make it clear and make it about you. It is also going to be imperative that you set yourself up for the next goals before you hit the first goals you are working for.

Goals? What Goals?!?

As I said earlier, for a while, I was not in the right mindset to set anything that sounded like goals, mission, or life vision. I could not even get out of bed let alone change the world. If the thought of making goals is too much for you, then do what I did. Ask yourself: what are some of the things that are happening in your life now that you just are not proud of?

Let us be honest and make them real by writing them down here:

1) ————————————————————————

2) ————————————————————————

3) ————————————————————————

4) ————————————————————————

This is the most genuine starting point you can imagine. You are going to reverse engineer it. How can you now turn these into goals that you can be truly proud of? You can be proud to say I no longer do (fill in the blank).

If you do not have anything in mind to set as a goal, then talk about an area of your life that causes you to feel that depression. What is something that brings you down that you can now work through and flip on its head? You can now allow it to be an elevation point in your life and not the other way around anymore. Whether you realize it or not, you just set a goal for yourself!

Be Specific!

You do not want to set a goal for yourself such as "I want to help more people." Some of the questions that will arise from that are: How many people do you want to help? How do you want to help them? What does it look like for them to be helped?

If you say, "I want to wake up earlier," then some questions are: What time is earlier? What will waking up at that time do for you? "I am going to wake up at 6 a.m. every day, and I am going to set two alarms, that way I have no choice in the matter. I have to get up to ensure I am able to start off the day winning." You need to get definitive with your goal statements!

For those of you who are like I was and maybe want to re-establish relationships, specifically for your significant others, what is that going to take? What do you need to do? What is a better relationship? It took me dating Stephanie all over again. I had to spend time with her and tell her I loved her so that she sincerely knew it because for a long time it just was not happening like that.

Communicating was part of my task list to achieve that goal. I had to tap into the small steps to achieve the goal. It is not just about wanting to achieve something. How are you going to break it down into small feasible steps that lead to the final destination?

Goals = Growth

Know in your mind you are going to need to have a new goal to set for yourself because, without it, you will have that lost feeling or that feeling of "what do I do now?" It is the elation from the accomplishment, then the crash because of lack of a next target. That is a very dangerous place to be because you can slide all the way back to square one if you are not careful. It is important, as you have a push toward a goal, that you know this is not going to be the only goal that you have. You are constantly going to be setting new and bigger goals.

You want to continue to expand your mind, expand your potential, do more, and do better. Maybe you have the same goal again but this time you want to do better and/or make the goal better.

Always Progressing

Remember, you do not need to run full steam ahead right away. You are in a continuous progression, and not everything is meant to be implemented immediately. Having a set schedule is imperative in starting this process. The second that you stop doing one thing, you can fall into that trap of failure when that is not a part of the exercises.

The point of these changes is to create a routine. It is about staying focused on your goal and how you are getting to that goal. You may have to make some tweaks, and that is ok! You pick what goals are right for you and implement them. Write your clear action steps that will allow you to hit those goals. Establish your system for measuring your progress. Every fifteen to thirty days, check in with yourself. Look at your plan and see what is working for you. How did March go in comparison to February? How do you plan on July being better than May? This is not a perfect science. This is something that is tailor-made to you. These are only tools that can help throughout your process.

By focusing on pushing toward your goals, you can move your life one step closer to being driven by your vision, your mission, and direction to be better. I was able to live my first goal, and now my new vision is to help tens of thousands, hundreds of thousands or millions of people worldwide demolish depression, annihilate anxiety, and pulverize PTSD in their lives.

In the next section, we are going to get crystal clear on what success should mean to you and how to define the term for your life.

STEP THREE: SUCCESS

Reframe Your Trauma + Rewrite Your Story

Reframing your trauma is extremely important because it allows you the opportunity to change the negative into a positive. That is the narrative that you continue to speak to yourself. It is what will allow you to start making steps in the right direction. You may get a certain diagnosis and you may think to yourself, "This is awful. What am I going to do?" It may be a career-altering diagnosis. But staying stuck in it will only drive you deeper into a depressed, anxiety-filled stress hole. By drawing up a new goal and vision for your life and seeing it as a positive path, you can begin to move forward and progress more quickly.

When you have the same thoughts in your mind that replay over and over, regardless of whether they are positive or negative, that is the story you will live by. If you consistently have the negative thoughts and feelings about certain instances in your life, that is what you will focus on. If you constantly feed your mind with positive thoughts and feelings, that is what you will live by. **Control your**

thoughts and you will control what is troubling you. By reframing your trauma into a positive thought, you will control it and it will no longer control you. By changing your personal narrative about your life, you will have a favorable and enthusiastic approach about how to live your life to be as successful as you possibly can.

Sometimes when you establish a goal, it can turn into something much bigger than expected and it can take longer than you initially set out for it to be. So there has to be an acknowledgement of if you do not reach your goal initially or immediately, that it is ok. You can call it a fail. You can call it a backfire, disaster, flop, bomb, or whatever you want. Whatever you call it, just know it does not mean the end of the world. Stephanie and I call it failing. Here is the important part to understand. **We fail forward fast.**

SUCCESS- the accomplishment of one's goals[13]

Failing is only defined by not surpassing the goal in the time you set out for it. However, if you look back, you are more than likely going to be farther than where you started out.

---

[13] "Success," Dictionary.com, Accessed 16 May 2020, https://www.dictionary.com/browse/success?s=t

Ask yourself, "How much progress did I make?" It may not be much, or it may be exponentially beyond what you imagined or gave yourself credit for. When we are talking about success, these are the opportunities that you take to stop, acknowledge where you were in comparison to where you are at now, and give yourself some grace and credit! If you hit the goal, then FANTASTIC! I am high fiving you right now for the effort and hard work displayed. That is amazing. It is also important to note that you will not always hit your goal. Period. When you don't, never feel bad or get down on yourself for it.

As long as you were pushing toward that goal and doing anything toward that goal, you were actually failing forward. That compounds over time. Set out on your next goal to achieve that goal you had before, but give it a new date and tweak your plans this time to be just a little bit different. Some minor tweaks just might be what you need to set yourself up for success this time around and achieve the goal.

**Success is...**

...only a word subject to personal interpretation. Always remember that. It is important to push. It is essential to move. It is crucial to have and work toward at least one piece of success every single day. Remember, I am only speaking from my own experience, and this is what I have to do every single day to beat the diagnosis/story that I was initially given. And when I say every day, I mean every single day. There are days when I lose; I'm just being absolutely transparent. The most important thing is now those days are very few and far between.

Success is really all about getting out of your comfort zone, working toward the goal, and measuring the goal. It is important when it comes to measuring to ensure you are using the same stick of measurement as before for evaluation. Otherwise, you are not getting the proper results. **Success can be simply you implementing part of your plan every single day.** That means you had a successful day every day. If part of your plan is you looked at your schedule the night before and you were able to see what you had scheduled for the next day and you actually woke up on time and got out of bed when you said you would, that is a success! Some days, that is as far as I got.

Woohoo! Maybe you did not do anything else on the list, but you did that. You have to give yourself credit for that success.

What if you had seven tasks to complete and you did all seven? Is that better or worse than doing only two? It is still a success no matter what numbers you are putting behind it. Acknowledge it, celebrate it and, most importantly, share your success with somebody. Share it with someone who understands that you have a goal for yourself. Have some accountability with somebody else outside that can really support you in the process. That goes back into the re-connecting aspect I spoke about earlier. It is one big positivity loop.

First Pieces of Success

My first piece of success was lifting the fog out of the house, so to speak. Opening up the windows and letting some fresh air in. Opening up the shutters and letting the light in the house was a big difference in just the feeling inside. It just progressed from there. Enjoying the park with the kids together. And that progressed to Stephanie and me having date nights again. Which progressed to something else and something bigger and something more challenging. It was literally climbing the ladder of success. **In your worst moments is the best time to change.**

That is when my trust and confidence grew. I knew in my heart that I could stretch out and go for a few really big goals in life because I was successful in the little things. Because you are deliberate about being successful in the little things, you can stretch.

I don't feel like I am successful because I wrote this book. I will feel more successful when you take this opportunity and this tool to make yourself better. That is my definition of success. That is me giving back and that is where I am feeling fulfillment. A lot of times, fulfillment and success are only found in what you have given someone else. A gift.

Your gifts and accomplishments should not be hoarded away and hidden. They should be shared with others to help them get better in life. Sharing your gift. Sharing your testimony. Sharing your message. Sharing how you have overcome life's battles. That is a huge part of success.

Your New System

We are talking about creating a new system for yourself. A system of accomplishment and success so that you are coming out of the negativity. You may still have negative thoughts throughout the day. I know I do. You may have moments where you feel defeated again or you still feel down. It's ok. We all do! When you start putting these tools into play and acknowledge the little successes, then you will start to make big progress.

For me, it was walking to the mailbox, taking the trash to the curb, dropping the kids off at school. Seems so laughable now, but it was huge at the time. I did it and I could acknowledge it. Instead of letting our toddlers know how mad I was when the milk was spilled yet again and making them feel scared and bad, it was a more calm and subdued response. You can't cry over spilled milk, literally. Clean it up and move along so the day isn't ruined over spilled milk. Those were successes. Small. Seemingly miniscule but packed with huge ramifications.

I can't begin to explain how important it is going to be for you to acknowledge success. Every single day. When you go back to evaluate yourself after one week, two weeks, or monthly—whatever you set for yourself—you have to acknowledge where your success was and how far you have come. That is what will tell you that you can accomplish this goal. That is what reinforces how you get there and reinforces being able to set up a bigger goal, knowing that you can be confident in yourself to achieve it.

You do not want to set yourself up for failure instead of success. If you can't get out of bed because of debilitating depression, anxiety, or stress, then how are you going to accomplish the goal of building a successful business? Let's get out of bed first. Now you are talking to yourself at step ten as opposed to step one. Step one does not understand what step ten does. By the time you get to that goal, where you are reflecting, and you will realize the last few months have been amazing in the house because you are now more proactive. You feel better and are accomplishing the little goals that you are setting out to do. Having a good day at home. Picking up the kids. Taking out the trash. Now the goals become part of your routine! Now that they are your routine, you can start setting yourself up for the next round of goals with much more confidence, focus, and excitement. You are a different person now.

I couldn't set myself a goal to write this book when I could not get out of bed. Imagine the steps it took to get here. I was in the deepest hole I had ever been in two years ago, and now I'm a published author with ZERO experience in writing! **I didn't set out to write a book. I set out to help people.** I thought if we could create something that would make it possible to raise awareness, destigmatize mental health issues, be able to tell our story, and create a path for others to live fruitful and meaningful lives, the pain we experienced as a family would be worth it. This just happened to be an avenue to do so. In the end, all of this means I'm now able to help a lot more people achieve their dream of mental clarity and live a life fulfilled. I tell my kids all of the time: There is an unlimited amount of ways to get to the same place. You are only limited by your imagination, your creativity, or your mindset.

Let's Change Our Mind

I knew I could succeed because of the little successes I was having every day and the little things I was doing to achieve my goals. The small pieces that I was successful in, tangible and intangible, have allowed me a different mindset. **The whole point of success is to change your mindset.** We are going to focus on the successful aspects of working toward our goals, not the parts that went wrong. By setting bigger goals now, it is going to create self-confidence and trust within yourself. When you can trust yourself to do something, you start to squash all the fears and all the doubts that play out in your head on the repeat cycle. As you conquer the little things and check off the small, daily tasks to reach your goal, they all add up and have a compound effect in your life. The more you do and the better you do at that, the more you build up your confidence level and the stronger you are to push. The harder you can go. The farther you can go. It increases your endurance, the capacity to endure the forces that are working against you. **It's not what you know, it's what you do.**

Your own mind may be telling you it is not possible. Your own self is saying you are too tired. You don't want to get up and do it because you don't like it or it hurts or it reminds you of something. I am not nor will I advocate for something that is not safe or healthy, but I am saying it is extremely important and imperative to be able to set yourself up for little daily successes and be able to measure what success you've had over the past time frame you give yourself to evaluate. You either achieve the goal, which is fantastic and should be celebrated, or you didn't hit the goal but you failed forward. You are no longer in the place you used to be. You are in a better place, and now you can reset that same goal but with some minor tweaks.

We never quit. Ever.

What It Means to Me

Change your story, change your life.
-Tony Robbins-

When I changed the story about what PTSD meant for me, it was all about changing my daily thought patterns and incorporating action steps! It was now crystal clear to me how to stop worrying about what I could not control and focus on how I could change my habits and emotions daily, because I saw I could focus on getting life back in order, starting with myself.

I also learned that you DON'T have to feel like you will suffer from PTSD, anxiety, depression, or stress forever. You need to focus on changing your daily habits instead and shoot for success on a small scale. I changed the way I thought of the diagnosis and took daily action to achieve success. That's when I realized that I had to look toward balancing my work life with being a husband and father, which was changing my thought pattern and acknowledging the positives in life daily—allowing me to be open to new career paths.

I wanted to be a firefighter, and then I got this diagnosis and my whole life changed. It became the first day of the rest of my life. I had to learn that things do not work out the way you anticipate them. In that, however, I found this great lesson in life that made me redefine my entire story of PTSD. That was my way of seeing past the forest and moving forward to a better future for my family and me.

It is essential to go after what you want when you want for as long and hard as you can. There will always be bumps and challenges in the road, no matter how much you plan for it. A simple no cannot stop your progress. **Hearing no means *not right now* or *find another way*, but it does not mean quit!** There are infinite ways and possibilities to get to the same goal. Learn to be resourceful. Learn how to utilize your resources. Always go for your dreams and let no one, especially yourself, deter you from them!

We Don't Compare

Remember, success is defined by what you define it as. Everyone's measuring sticks are different. Do not get caught up in this comparison society that we have now by comparing your success with what society deems as "successful." Just because Billy got a brand-new truck does not mean he is successful. Suzy remodeled her kitchen? So what! Your success is measured by you. No one else! I was extremely successful in my mind because I made Steph laugh four times on a Tuesday. It had nothing to do with anyone else and had everything to do with me. Comparison to anyone or anything else is just a trap. Getting caught in that can bring you all the way back down to square one if you are not careful. Do not get caught in that comparison aspect of things when you are looking to define what success means to you, not what success means to society.

Howdy Partner!

Ensure that your accountability partner who you are sharing your success with understands why that success is so important to you and they're not comparing it to what it is that they feel is successful. They need to be at least an equal or higher level of what you are looking to accomplish. If you are choosing a partner to share these successes with, they need to at least be able to relate with what you are trying to accomplish and they understand the importance of it to you. You need someone who will champion for you. You want them to be honest. They are not going to tear you down. They are there to give you some critiques in a very deliberate way to help you get to your goal.

There are more than likely certain qualities, points, or characteristics in your life that you already know do well for you and things that you may have applied in your past that were positive but you have since gone astray on. Seeing it from someone else's perspective can possibly give you the clarity of mind to know or say to yourself that you should probably go back to a few of those things again. Or maybe it will prompt you to work on specific areas in life a bit more because you want to see success for those parts of your life. Reading it can be even better for you because you can highlight parts, jot down notes, re-read specific parts, and use them over and over.

I am highlighting how success factors into your ability to set new goals with a bigger vision and a bigger stretch and will allow for more accomplishments in the future because the little successes will compound for you. That also leads to an opportunity to give more. As you create more success, you are able to share with someone who is a few steps behind you or is just starting on their mental health journey. Either way, you were in their shoes not too long ago, so pay it back tenfold! It could be in your area of expertise. It could be with anxiety and depression. It could be with how to run a race, expand your business, etc. Whatever it may be, you are now in the position to compress someone else's timeframes and help them through what could be a perilous journey.

We have now hit on three of the four points of PTSD. In the next chapter, we are going to talk about why daily progress and work is so important in success.

STEP FOUR: DAILY

Rebuild Yourself + Take It One Day at a Time

You have to fight for the life you want.
-Dr. Sam Bakhtiar-

Every day, you start with a clean slate. Start fresh every day regardless of what happened the day before. When you wake up, you have a new opportunity to attack the day with full force and improve on the day before. You have a chance to reflect on what happened yesterday. Did you meet your goals? How productive were you? Did you stick to your schedule? You have a chance to adjust your action steps to make tomorrow more fruitful and positive.

When you think of daily action steps, think of reinforcing your new system or routine.

Daily- of, done, occurring, or
Issued each day or each weekday[14]

---

[14] "Daily," Dictionary.com, Accessed 16 May 2020, https://www.dictionary.com/browse/daily?s=t

It's helpful to regularly ask yourself, "What actions did I take that moved me closer to my desired success?" The patterns and routines you create and commit to in your daily life are the key drivers that will push you toward success daily. If brushing your teeth regularly is your first goal, then awesome! If you can get that down once or twice a day when that was not a regular pattern before, look forward to that. From there, see what else you can add to the list that will change your trajectory. As you re-evaluate as you progress, start adding to your list.

Practice Makes Perfect

You need to ask yourself regularly going forward how you feel in a moment. Can you improve the way you are feeling, and if so, what will it take to do that? If you do not like the way you feel in that very moment, then stop, take some deep breaths, ground your feet, and center yourself. Remember you have two feet. Feel your two feet. Focus on your breathing. Hear your heartbeat. Allow the feeling to take its time and get washed away. Do not come out until you feel like your state has improved. It does not matter how long it takes. **This is a muscle that needs to be exercised, and you can and will get better with it over time.** It took me a long time to feel myself shift, but I got much better at this exercise because I had a ton of practice. And I mean a ton of practice.

Let's Write

There were plenty of times when writing this book that recall brought me back to these moments in time that I had already gotten through; it does not mean my memory has faded, though. I am still going back to that same routine of how to get out of those feelings and emotions. There was no lack of days that I had to call Steph during my writing process and ask her to help me out of the hole I was sinking back into. It is as simple as her speaking positive affirmations over me, telling me to get up and move about, and, most importantly, take a step back. I had to reset myself, then proceed with the task at hand. It would not be a simple five-minute reset, however. Sometimes it took me an hour or so, and that is ok! Give yourself the grace needed but NOT excuses. Totally different pieces to a puzzle.

Say you are new to exercising and want to get in shape. You set out to run/ walk 1 mile but you become fatigued and stop short of the goal. Give yourself some grace with that! You still went out and put one foot in front of the other. If you continue to set out to run/ walk the same 1 mile consistently, do you think you will accomplish your goal? Absolutely! Now, if day by day goes by and you continue to not go out there and try but you have different reasons as to why, those are excuses! See the difference? Grace is good, just do not allow grace to become excuses.

Even today with continuous daily work on myself, when I start to feel that turn back, like my body is turning me backward and twisting me from my course, these little things allow me to reset and get back on track. Breathing and centering myself, talking to my accountability partner, taking a step back, and removing myself from the situation are just a few new tools in my tool belt I utilize daily.

Music has a huge influence on my state also. I cannot tell you how often in a day I just put on some headphones, find some space in a room or my car, and turn it up full blast and yell. It is normally upbeat and awesome. I have a playlist that I always go to, and I just hit shuffle. It will not matter which song comes on because I am ready for whatever one it is. No longer than five minutes of singing, dancing, and increasing my heart rate and I am in a completely different state. Make sure if you try this that you are completely unapologetic. Just let loose and have fun! We as a family do this often. "Dance party" is what we call it. Everyone has to get up and participate. **Allow your mind, body, and spirit the freedom it deserves to explode!**

Daily Means...

Let us be mindful. You are ensuring you have your schedule laid out for the day. You are ensuring you are including all of the basic necessities to live. You are going to layer over time more things that will add value to your life and can now become autopilot after twenty-one, sixty, ninety days, or however long each task takes to become a habit. **Make it a habit.** Then you will be able to continue to add more things to make certain you keep traveling the path of success with wellness mentally and physically.

When I say daily, I mean it very literally. Daily. Life's challenges are going to throw something at you every day. Sometimes it may be the same thing over and over. Those are constant tests to see if you can and will pass. If you keep getting the same trials repetitively, then maybe you are not passing them the right way and life will keep giving them to you until you figure it out. Then it is another different test. You are either leaving a challenge, in a challenge, or walking into a challenge! The question is how are you going to handle it?

If your schedule goes off one day, are you going to let it affect your next day? If you miss a day of your movement routine, is that going to mess you up for the whole week? You have to remember: compounding works both negatively AND positively.

Small, Smart Choices + *Consistency* + *Time*
= *RADICAL DIFFERENCES*
- Darren Hardy -

Every day is a clean slate regardless of your successes or failures the day before. But the momentum of success the previous day will give you a bit of an edge. If you had success the day before, you will see and feel a change in your demeanor in the morning. That feeling of positive momentum is so huge. That feeling of positivity as opposed to not.

Just know that everything is not going to be perfect. I have plenty of days that I still struggle. There might be a few days consecutively where you just have a feeling of **UGGHHH,** and that is ok. Those are the most important days to reach out and connect via phone call or face to face with someone. Those are the crucial days to move your body, to eat well, and hydrate.

If you feel like junk and you perpetuate it with bad eating, isolation, and negative self-talk, it will only allow you to slip back into the cycle you are pushing hard to escape from. You do not want to get to the "I'll figure it out" or "it'll pass" stage.

You are not addicted to working out and exercising. You are addicted to the feeling you have after you work out. Similarly, you are not addicted to opening up and sharing or making and answering that phone call. But you are addicted to that feeling of knowing that someone cares about you, is there to listen, or that you have the opportunity for help after that call is made. After that activity is done. **It is the outcome, not the action.**

Filtering

When issues or challenges start to aggravate me and I start to get upset and react, my blow-up phase is a lot less and a lot shorter than it used to be. Being consciously aware of issues that are starting to piss you off and are probably going to instigate you yelling is a very important tool to have in your daily arsenal as well. What are you doing or going to do to shut it down? I talked about one of the hard body reset tools I do with breathing and grounding myself. Before, I would have told somebody off, fired somebody, or cut off a relationship completely. But knowing that my mind was deceiving me into thinking the worst and I am already aware of it, I can now stop, breathe, and refrain from raging. That is from daily practice by facing the challenges that come head on. We are destroying the habit of escaping. Face it. Handle it. Triumph over it. Celebrate. No one has ever won a battle by running the other way.

It is important to have your own tools to use if you do not use the ones I suggest. It does not matter exactly what you do, just do it with intent.

This is your life that you are pushing to improve every day, so develop, shift, create, adjust, arrange, re-arrange, etc.

MOVING FORWARD

If you can't fly then run. If you can't run then walk.
If you can't walk, then crawl. But whatever you do, you
have to keep moving forward.
- Dr. Martin Luther King Jr.

People ask me all the time how I was able to walk away from my career as a professional firefighter that I worked so hard for. I tell them, even with my PTSD, that I still feel lucky. God allowed me the opportunity to live my dream. So many people in society today can't even say that they know what their vision is, let alone have lived out their dream once, and I have had the opportunity to do that. I also tell them, even though treating my PTSD meant walking away from my past life, it also meant embracing a new life and a new dream. It gave me a new chance to live out a new goal, vision, and mission in my life. That journey has led me into seasons of growth and opportunity that I never would have imagined I would experience.

You are only going to feel your best, move your best, and perform your best when you pour into yourself. Period. I have to remind Stephanie just like she reminds me that it is ok to be selfish about certain circumstances in life. If she is not at her best, then she cannot be her best for us and vice versa. It is imperative to allow yourself a time and place to breathe. Every day that you do more, read more, and focus on yourself more is an opportunity for you to be your best for yourself and everyone around you. **If my PTSD journey has taught me anything, it's that life is about growth, development, and learning to live with the complexities of life.**

What can you do?

We are here to start a conversation. The fact that we can write our own story, have control over it, and open up about our life is extremely empowering. It makes us think how many people have areas of their lives that they absolutely refuse to talk about, the one or few things that they feel like they are holding close to their chest. In all actuality, that thing is probably the piece of your life that is holding you back from truly living free. It may be holding you captive without you even understanding the negative impact it has on you daily.

> Do you think about it every day?
>
> Do you deal with it every day?
>
> Do you hate to share or talk about it?
>
> Does it stir up a lot of emotions?
>
> Do you know why?

These are questions that you should ask yourself. Now the question I have for you.

If you conquered your fear, shared it, and were able to empower one other person, would it be worth it?

Just Move!

Moving forward for us looks like us truly believing that this movement we are building will impact lives around the world in a positive way. It is that simple. This project is something that has me the most excited I have been in years. The person I was would have never imagined being able to impact people positively with my story because I was just trying to survive the day. Flight or fight mode was all that I knew for a very long time. **It was not until I picked to fight over taking flight that I began to rebuild myself into the person I am becoming.** It is a daily battle to manage my emotional state that I know in my heart and mind that I am now winning.

You are not going to have LONG days anymore. That has such a negative connotation. You are going to have structured days. Meaningful days. Fruitful days. Successful days! Every day you need to be fighting to get better, be more for yourself and your family, and surpass any success beyond your wildest imagination. But first, let's fight to get out of bed. One step at a time.

Moving forward is hope, encouragement, and continuing to see your life in a positive way. That is the ultimate vision. We walked through steps to get you through little to medium to big goals in your life. Continue to follow these steps in life to keep pushing toward success daily. Do not neglect the small things you do every day. They are the stepping-stones to a solid foundation that you stand on to achieve higher peaks in life.

Let's talk about something greater than today or tomorrow

Let's work on your long-term goals, vision, or mission.

Where do you want your life to be in three years?

Five years?

Ten years?!?

You don't want to be in the same place you are now, which is why you have taken the time to get this far in the book. High five!!! We will talk about what goal setting in the long term looks like. Financially. Physically. Mentally. Spiritually. Emotionally. Which one of these is the pain point in your life? The one piece that if you get right will open you up to things beyond imagination?

Listen, five years ago is when my symptoms started. I was in the worst place in my life. I sought help. I was given a diagnosis of PTSD, anxiety, and depression. I figured out the steps that I needed to take to get out of that place, all the while knowing I wanted to be financially successful with my family, but also enjoying my time with them again.

That is where we are now. It is a five-year fast forward. My life is completely changed. My career has changed drastically. I have new opportunities because I WANT new opportunities. **I have new opportunities because my life has evolved, and I have a bigger vision and mission for myself and my family now.** For that reason, I am doing things differently now. I am open to doing things differently, and I am open to trying something new that I essentially would not have done prior to this happening. This is where it is ok to stretch your vision. I am giving you permission to go wild with the vision that you have for yourself. When you have that greater, long-term vision out there, that is when you are going to stretch more and recognize those opportunities right in front of you. You can push yourself further and stretch yourself more when it comes to reaching for your extended vision and mission.

You Can't Eat the Elephant Whole

There is a well-known riddle that asks the question *"How do you eat an elephant?"* The answer? *"One bite at a time."* And it's the same with our lives. You can change your life one moment, one thought, or one step at a time. You may not be able to accomplish all of your goals or get past your mental challenges in one day, but you can break it down into small, manageable tasks that will get you to the overall finish line.

This is a 12,000-foot view of your land. We are future casting here. We can break it down into bite-size chunks. How about setting up an evaluation for every quarter? Treat this like a business. Every three months, block off a day, go to your most favorite place in the world to think, and have an honest session with yourself. Look at both the good and bad. Positive and negative. Easy and difficult times that you have had. Celebrate the positive and push to eliminate the negatives.

You do not want to leave this earth with regret. You do not want to be in old age saying, "I wish I would have tried...," or "I wish I would have done..." This is where you open your eyes to your new awakening, your new-found vision for your life, and how much more you can benefit from daily habits and successes. Now I am in a position to help you who may be in exactly the same shoes I have been in for the last five years. I can help you to see success in your life again. For me, that is fulfilling. How can you start to feel fulfilled?

Do you want to help people in lower socio-economic areas?

> Do you want to start a school food program to make sure kids are fed in order to get a good education?

> Are you looking to put clothes on people's backs?

> Are you passionate for homeless individuals and families?

> Are you passionate to help others with the same types of diagnosis as you?

Pushing Toward Success Daily is all about reaching those little successes so you can achieve that greater success that is burning in your soul. I also want to help you to constantly have the perspective of moving forward, future casting, doing things above and beyond just today, for tomorrow and the rest of your life.

LETTER FROM A SPOUSE

I will never forget the night we met. A mutual best friend was hanging out at Shannon's apartment and invited me over to catch up. Little did I know that I would spend little to no time speaking with our mutual friend. Shannon and I spent several hours getting to know each other by exchanging stories about our careers and travels. He was so fascinating and seemed like such a good catch. I just had the impression he was taken, and at the end of the night, I went home without exchanging any information with him. It was about a week later that Shannon started calling weekly for about a month until he stopped. I was surprised because I didn't give him my number, but he seemed to enjoy calling. I had just seen that movie *He's Just Not That Into You* and thought, "Well, he must have moved on."

Fast forward two months, and I found out Shannon was hired on to his dream job with LAFD. I was happy to hear the news from another mutual friend, but I was perturbed he didn't tell me himself. So, the excellent communicator I am decided to call him and congratulate him. That call led to a lunch meeting that turned into an at-home movie, a college basketball game on TV, and eventually a Lakers game. We are both sports fans, so that was a significant plus. Our lunch meeting ended with his mom's leftover casserole for dinner, and then I went home. About ten minutes into my drive home, he asked if I could turn around and come back. He was half-serious, and I was half-serious about considering it. For the next month, we began seeing each other as often as our schedules permitted. A little more than a month later, he asked me to move in, and within seven months, he had asked my parents for permission to marry me. Now, neither set of parents was on board with the fast-paced move in, but they loved us and respected our commitment to each other.

As I write about our journey, we have celebrated more than ten years as a couple and nine years married, and two beautiful and smart children have been a part of our journey. I have always heard from other married couples that marriage takes work. Up until maybe year three, life seemed pretty sweet. After our son was born, I began to notice that Shannon's patience level was very short. This was very different from the man I married. I chalked it up to him being tired from work and studying for his bachelor's degree.

After a while, it began to take a toll on the kids and me. The short temper turned into fights and arguments over the littlest things. The conflicts with me made me feel like I should give him his space and let him rest. I also took note that the kids didn't want to be around him. So, as often as I could, I would take our two toddlers out to just about anywhere. We would frequent Disneyland for two to three hours, only the three of us. We also attended family events without Shannon to give him rest and space. It seemed like the right thing to do at the time.

I had adjusted my attitude to be ready for a disagreement, fight, and lack of willingness to participate on Shannon's end so that I would not overreact to him or get disappointed. This was how I coped. This was how I made sure our children were happy. It wasn't all bad. We laughed and had good times, too; however, it took massive amounts of work. I relied heavily on my mother-in-law to help with childcare while I worked at the hospital so that the kids were in a positive environment, even when Shannon was off work and at home.

The day finally came in late August 2016 that Shannon asked for help. He came to me and said he wasn't feeling like himself and thought he should speak with someone and take some time off of work. This was coming from a guy who rarely asked for help and only took time off for vacations. I was shocked and so relieved all at the same time. My reaction was I was going to do whatever it took to support him. I knew at that moment that the road ahead would not be easy; however, I was going to be Shannon's wife for better or worse. Our vows had already been tested through the arguments and distance that was created between us. This was something different, though. I knew I was going into battle, so to speak, for my husband, for our marriage, and our family.

The next steps came in the form of Shannon seeking out help from his employee assistance program through work. He was able to have a sit down before being tested/quizzed on how he was feeling. Through that experience, we learned he was challenged with depression and anxiety. Hallelujah! We had a name for this behavior, and it felt like I saw the light at the end of the tunnel. It also meant within a few months, Shannon would be diagnosed with PTSD after counseling sessions and further evaluation. That was great because now we could learn more about how to cope and begin to heal as a family. It also meant Shannon was leaving his dream job because, at that time, he could not bear going back to work. I was so conflicted. I was happy for us to know the why behind the behavior and terrified to watch him walk away from a position he loved to his core. I encouraged him to wait for as long as his employer would allow before turning in his badge. This was the ultimate sacrifice on his end to improve our family life. I don't know who had a harder time with that: him or me. Either way, we were moving forward together.

My takeaways from this experience as a spouse/domestic partner/family member/best friend:

- If the behavior of your loved one is changing over a prolonged amount (more than just a few days/weeks) of time and communication is suffering, it is okay to check in and ask if anything else is going on.

- It is good to seek help for yourself by having someone you can confide in, whether that is a best friend, a close family member who does not allow gossip, or a counselor.

- Often, resources may be available that you may not have considered, such as your employer or your spouse/domestic partner's employer via employee assistance programs, counseling sessions through a health plan, and even your local place of worship.

- Last, you never have to be alone or suffer in silence. Seeking help for yourself or your loved one is truly a sign of strength in my eyes.

It is so crucial for me to share about what betrayal looked like for me. Here I have been a nurse for years and have taken an entire semester on psychiatric nursing in nursing school, as well as psychology classes for my bachelor's degree requirements. Yet, none of my training or studies kicked in to make me think for one minute that my husband was experiencing anxiety and depression. After thinking about it, I realized that the signs were there, but I didn't know how to read them. It's as if I was driving in a foreign country. I could see the signs; I just didn't know what they meant. I knew about a few traumatic incidents he experienced as a firefighter; I also knew he sometimes had terrible nightmares, but it never translated to PTSD for me. Daily drinking, a short temper, a lack of desire to participate in family outings: those were all signs. So, when he was diagnosed, I thought to myself, "How did I miss this? Why did I make this about me?" Before the diagnosis, my thought was maybe I didn't make him happy anymore, or perhaps he didn't really like being a family man. These were thoughts I kept to myself for a long time, instead of checking on him to see how he was feeling.

As Shannon felt like his mind had betrayed him, I knew it was my time to step up and hold faithful to my vows I made as his wife. For the first time, I was seeing my "superhuman" husband vulnerable. My focus and concern became advocating for him to receive the resources and help he needed to feel whole again. In all honesty, I had no idea what the journey ahead looked like, who to call first, or how long this journey would take. What I did know with certainty was that, by the grace of God, we would get through this together.

As a family member, I was allowed to be a part of some of Shannon's appointments, but not all. There were times where he seemed frustrated with going to therapy appointments alone. To be honest, I was a little frustrated that I couldn't be there too. My nature is to fix things, keep the peace, and help. I had to embrace the fact that I could be an encourager and allow him to take the necessary steps needed for therapy. He also shared on multiple occasions that he was tired of recounting the memories or talking about his feelings, and he just wanted to move on. What I knew was there was a process that needed to happen for him to receive proper assistance. My job was to listen, or sit quietly with him, and encourage him that we were going to get through it together. He needed to know I would be by his side every step of the way.

As a part of this journey, there was an incredible shift in Shannon's nature, so unbelievable it drew us closer to each other. It was as though he finally let his guard down after a long while, and we could really laugh again. The reality was that I needed to step up as a wife, mother, and household provider. I increased my hours at work to carry our family with medical benefits, as well as ensure that the bills were paid and our business continued to run well. I needed to operate at peak performance levels in every area of my life. I could see that this role was a season for me to get through, not a lifetime. To some, this may sound tough, but it wasn't, because I was walking in my purpose. As I reflect, the tradeoff was worth it. I was slowly getting the great qualities of the man I married back.

As time marched forward and appointments for Shannon grew in number, I could see Shannon trusted me. Shannon was beginning to put his trust in God again, as well. We had attended church together regularly throughout our marriage, but I could tell something was missing for Shannon. I prayed for strength for myself, I prayed for healing for Shannon, and I prayed that our relationship as a family of four would be renewed. Some days there were many tears, some days I would scream in the car when I was alone, but most days, I would play music and sing at the top of my lungs in praise. The singing still happens most days; my days with tears are much fewer and further between. I feel a whole new experience of joy in my life. Has it been rainbows and butterflies? Gosh, no! My faith, indeed, has been my strength. I know not everyone reading this will agree with our faith, but it is genuinely a part of our journey, and so I believe it is essential to share. We were living out what seemed to be our toughest battle in life together, yet we were able to sustain and grow. That, to me, is a God thing.

My takeaways:

- Just because you may be in the healthcare or mental healthcare fields does not always mean you know what someone you love is experiencing.
- When a loved one needs help, it may mean we need to readjust our position, that may mean at home, work, or as emotional support.

- It is vital to have a safe space for yourself, to vent, breathe, meditate, pray, etc.

Your faith, even as small as a mustard seed, can carry you through even the most difficult times.

It took about four or five months of Shannon's leave of absence for him to adjust to our new normal. He was becoming the primary care provider of our home and our children's daily activities. I was able to remain focused on working at the hospital and on our business. Most importantly, the relationship between Shannon and our children shifted from never calling for Daddy to only calling for Daddy. Some moms may feel that gut punch of being less favored. For me, I teared up with joy, knowing that their relationship was being restored.

There was a day that Shannon finally said to me that he was okay with me talking about "it." I had been feeling a tug at my heart to share this experience with others because I really felt that Shannon's story might have a positive impact on the life of at least one family. My first share was in a private social media group. I wish I could say it went well, but sadly I cannot. The post was removed, and I felt angry, vulnerable, appalled. What I didn't think of was how this taboo subject would come across to others in this group. I thought of the positive outcome that could happen by having a candid conversation, without thinking of how some people perceive this subject to be repulsive, too close to home, or too sad to stop and think about.

From that day on, I decided I could not take it personally if people did not want to talk about our story. The best I could do was share the positives that came about from Shannon asking for help, and if people were open to hearing more, I would share more. To my surprise, the number of supportive responses from friends and family grew. The part I appreciate the most is the follow-up questions and those friends of Shannon's who still reach out and remain close to him. Those friends are heroes to me because they didn't abandon their friend when times got tough.

To be quite frank, mental health tends to be a stigmatized subject for most. Someone with a mental health diagnosis doesn't require a bandage, cast, sling, crutches, or necessarily show on the outside what is happening on the inside. I believe that this may be a reason why some people have a hard time understanding a diagnosis like anxiety or depression or other mental health issues. With Shannon, he has always been the life of the party, animated, and a little louder than everyone else, with a big smile and an infectious laugh. We had family, friends, and co-workers who couldn't believe that Shannon was dealing with depression and anxiety. For this reason, it became apparent that the next phase of this season we were in was to be bolder about sharing with others. What transpired for us was a course of healing, and that told me loud and clear that there is hope for others going through this.

This empathy has come from my personal experiences. There were times in my life before Shannon, and while I was with Shannon, that gave me a glimpse into the feelings of depression and anxiety. I cared for critically ill and dying children for almost six years. There are children and families that I used to see in my dreams. I will never forget them or the pain that they faced, and the deep emotions it stirred within me. I was briefly married and divorced at a young age, and many people didn't know. It still left me with a feeling of shame and isolation for about a year following that. I had to make changes in my life to overcome that. I was also in an accident that totaled my car and left me in back pain, but the worst part for me was the anxiety I had from being in a car for the next year following that incident. With that said, Shannon and I both recognize that there are so many people who are young and old who experience loss, separation from ones they love, traumatic incidents, and so on that are not associated with the letters PTSD.

That forced me to stop and think about what I could share with others based on my experience as a supportive loved one. So, throughout the last few years, I became the primary head of the household financially and stepped up where I needed to. There was a missing piece that got left behind about one to two years after Shannon had asked for help. That was my concern to care for my health. I had been taking care of myself by working out and eating well consistently until things started to feel comfortable. I began to eat very unhealthy food very often and stopped working out altogether as comfort mechanisms. After about a year of this, I recognized what I was doing to myself, how it was making me feel, and all the new clothes I needed to buy as a result. Now, I have loved myself at every size, but I have not always felt the same about walking a flight of stairs at every size. As a nurse, I know the repercussions of being overweight on overall health. I decided to do what our flight attendants advise before takeoff: I put the oxygen mask on myself first. It was time to make me and my health a priority again so I could continue to show up at 100 percent in the other areas of my life.

My example above is an illustration of how I must keep myself in check to be my best. For some people, the oxygen mask may be getting their finances in order, keeping their alcohol consumption down, painting, meditating, going to the beach, playing an instrument, or just directly talking to someone else. When Shannon said he was changing what PTSD meant to him and now considers it as Pushing Toward Success Daily, I fell in love with that meaning. The way I push is by working out at least four to five times per week. Toward is the goal I have chosen to maintain my weight, and that requires a healthy nutrition plan. Success to me comes in many forms; it includes finishing my workouts strong, seeing my children smile and laugh, listening to Shannon crack up at my goofy jokes. Daily is just that. I strive to move daily, make mostly healthy choices daily, and maintain my sense of humor and show kindness to others daily. Again, this is based on my needs, and this can be tailored to yours as well.

As far as being a support for Shannon now, I have learned how to read his signs. When he begins to get extra bossy or stops allowing the kids to make simple choices or becomes quiet at a get-together, then I check in. Sometimes he needs a reminder to adjust his behavior, or I gently ask if he is doing okay. Our communication has become so good that a quick turnaround takes place. We went from arguing and fighting to communicating and getting back to a healthy relationship.

My takeaways:

- We can destigmatize mental health issues by being open to learn as well as listen.

- To change, you must change things.

- Pushing Toward Success Daily is something available to everyone.

- When you take the time to learn the signs, you may be able to deescalate a situation before it becomes a full-blown disaster.

ENDNOTES

Chris Foy, "The Reasons Your Loved One with PTSD is Self-Isolating." August 29, 2019
https://fherehab.com/learning/reasons-ptsd-self-isolating/

"Daily," Dictionary.com, Accessed 16 May 2020,
https://www.dictionary.com/browse/daily?s=t

"Do I really need to drink 8 glasses of water a day?" One Medical,
https://www.onemedical.com/blog/live-well/daily-water-intake/

"Goal," Dictionary.com, Accessed 16 May 2020,
https://www.dictionary.com/browse/goal?s=t

"How Much Sleep Do We Really Need: Revisited," National Sleep Foundation,
https://www.sleepfoundation.org/articles/how-much-sleep-do-we-really-need

"How to Deal with a Spouse Who Has PTSD Nightmares," Sleep.org, 2020,
https://www.sleep.org/articles/deal-with-spouse-ptsd-nightmares/

Jamie Wiebe, "5 Ways to Strengthen Your Support System," 10 April 2019, https://www.talkspace.com/blog/how-to-strengthen-your-support-system/

Mary Jane, "9 Tips to Measure and Control Portion Sizes," 19 November 2018, https://www.healthline.com/nutrition/portion-control#section3

"Mental Health by the Numbers," National Alliance on Mental Illness, September 2019, https://www.nami.org/learn-more/mental-health-by-the-numbers

"Push," Dictionary.com, Accessed 16 May 2020, https://www.dictionary.com/browse/push

"Success," Dictionary.com, Accessed 16 May 2020, https://www.dictionary.com/browse/success?s=t

"The Water in You: Water and the Human Body," U.S. Geological Survey, https://www.usgs.gov/special-topic/water-science-school/science/water-you-water-and-human-body?qt-science_center_objects=0#qt-science_center_objects

"Toward," Dictionary.com, Accessed 16 May 2020, https://www.dictionary.com/browse/toward?s=t

<u>*9 Daily Action Steps Example*</u>

4 AM	*Wake Up*
4:15-5 AM	*Prayer/Meditation*
5:15 AM	*Exercise Routine*
6:30 AM	*Positive Self-Grooming*
7 AM	*Kids to School*
8:30 AM	*Work Day*
3 PM	*Kids from School*
5 PM	*Family Time*
7 PM	*Dinner*
8 PM	*Kids Bedtime*
8:30 PM	*Phone Call*
9 PM	*Self-development*
10 PM	*Bedtime*

9 Daily Action Steps

Time of Day	Your 9 Daily Action Steps

Self-Development Questionnaire

1. What is something that you have always wanted to learn about?

2. Where are certain areas in your life you feel you want to improve?

3. What do you like about your life?

4. Are you prepared to change?

5. What are your values? What are your non-negotiables?

6. What is the most important thing to you?

7. How far will you get with your current daily routine?

8. Where can you add more FUN in your life?

9. What makes you feel alive?

10. Are you living your life or just having a life?

Life Assessment

Initial Daily Life Assessment	Scale 1-10
Food Intake	
Sleep Pattern	
Schedule/Work	
Relationships	
Exercise Routine	
Mindfulness	
Self-Development	

Rate yourself and be brutally honest with how you are doing in these areas. It will show you how structured your life is as well as areas you may be suffering in. If you are a 5 or below in any area, that is where you need to focus your efforts to improve. It is crucial to not lose focus in areas you may be excelling in.

<u>Goals</u>

My goal is:

My time frame for my goal is:

My reasons for pushing toward this goal are:

My action steps to achieve my goal are:

I will know that I achieved my goal when:

When I reach my destination, I will celebrate by: